Endorsements

When God releases fresh revelation of a dormant spiritual truth, He always begins with the Scriptures, unveiling insights yet unseen. He then follows this by refining and expanding our understanding through the process of application, much like a doctor's residency. I assure you; this progression has been walked out in Tom Schlueter's understanding of what he appropriately calls *Tribunals: The Authority of the Ekklesia to Legislate*. He has studied it; he has done it. If every state had someone leading its prayer initiatives with this level of understanding, we would see America transformed in a very short time.

Apostle Dutch Sheets
Dutch Sheets Ministries
GiveHim15

My friend Tom Schlueter, in this new book, has drawn a line in the sand. His book *Tribunals* clearly and precisely gives us spiritual understanding of the Ekklesia functioning in the highest level of God's authority. Tom, in his strength and grace, has brought forth spiritual understanding that will further equip and empower God's Ekklesia. As you read the words upon the pages of this book you will find a very clear and focused view of how the Legislative Branch of God's church, the Ekklesia, is to function. Susan and I, having the honor of being friends with Tom and Kay, can assure you that Tom has not written theory on the pages of *Tribunals*. We have seen and experienced the fleshing out of his insight. I encourage you to not only read this book but purchase several copies and give it to leaders you know. They will experience life and a fresh wind of authority to blow into their life and ministry. Tom, thank you for a job well done!

Apostle Clay Nash
Clay Nash Ministries

It is an honor to endorse *Tribunals*, written masterfully by my friend, Tom Schlueter. The revelation, wisdom, and insight that God has given him to help guide the Ekklesia will enable us all to reference this book as a resource in the coming days as we continue to move into our authority under Him. Thank you, Tom...well done!

Dr. Tim Sheets, Apostle
The Oasis Church
Middletown, Ohio

This read will change your prayer life because it expresses the heart of Kingdom authority, which Dr. Schlueter walks in with excellence. It also carries the Kingdom priority of relationship and being authentic. In every season our Father calls us to a new maturity corporately as well as individually. In *Tribunals*, Tom addresses maturing in identity, rest and purpose while breaking old wineskin paradigms. You will finish this read with a new enthusiasm, confidence, and heart cry to be who you are called to be and change the world! Let's do this!

Apostle Merrie Cardin
Founder and Leader of the Brazos Strategic Network
Apostolic leader of Brazos Covenant Ministries

Reading through this now, revelatory message that Tom has exceptionally scribed in *Tribunal: The Authority of the Ekklesia to Legislate*, I am overjoyed, challenged, and greatly inspired. I have known Tom and Kay for many years and have had the privilege and honor to partner with them in strategic and legislative intercession. I have witnessed firsthand and participated in the glory anointed, Holy Spirit directed and led tribunal gatherings. I have rejoiced seeing the resulting, tangible, measurable, Kingdom of Heaven, history-making breakthroughs, and victories. Friends, the message contained in this book shares great scriptural truths, impartation, activating steps and faith building and regional transformational testimonies that will empower you as the Kingdom of Heaven Ekklesia to see spiritual victories and transformation realized and manifest. As you engage in this Kingdom revelation you will see "His Kingdom, His will be done on earth as it is in Heaven." Thank you, Tom, for your obedience and faithfulness in pioneering this key revelation for this historic time of awakening and transformation.

Rebecca Greenwood
President and Co-founder
Christian Harvest International
Strategic Prayer Apostolic Network

Tom Schlueter has a legacy in Texas regarding changing a state through "prayer" and strategic action. This book lays out a Word based as well as a Holy Spirit breathed unique and successful way of leading a state into victory, area by area. Tom is a great leader, full of integrity as well as a God given heart for his assignment. This book will help you see fresh ways of moving your strategic territorial assignment into greater victory.

Barbara J Yoder
Founding and Overseeing Apostle
Shekinah Christian Church
www.shekinahchurch.org

Tribunals   **Dr. Thomas Schlueter**

Tribunals is an "in season" book. There is so much change and so many voices that it takes real hunger and real discernment to know what is of the Holy Spirit and the Scriptures and what is from simply soulish efforts that sound good on the surface. *Tribunals* is indeed of the Holy Spirit and of Scriptural Truth! Tom has done a great job communicating and clarifying the prophetic and the practical! Tribunals will cause you to re-appraise many of our comfortable perspectives that are now have simply become "old wineskins". *Tribunals* will be make you more dangerous to the forces of darkness than ever before. Sit down with your Bible, read *Tribunals*, let the hunger in your heart guide you. Let God move in your heart until a new wineskin has formed inside of you. Drink of the new wine of fresh Biblical understanding of the authority of Christ who IS reigning and ruling and partnering with his Ekklesia to bring a release of HIS authority through us as His Ekklesia that we have not understood before. "And of *the increase of His Kingdom* there shall no end..." (Isaiah 9:7).

Bob Long
Rally Call Ministries
Rally Call Leadership Network

Dr. Tom Schlueter has presented the heart and mind of King Jesus for the twenty-first-century church. The truths Tom shares from the Bible and personal life experiences will challenge the Ekklesia to demonstrate the kingdom of God and transform their areas of influence. This book could be the catalyst that begins the fulfillment of Christ's purpose for the kingdoms of this world to become the kingdom of our God and His saints. *Tribunals, The Authority of the Ekklesia to Legislate* will shift you into new paradigms of experiencing transformation and becoming a reformer who takes territory!

Tom lives what he writes. He's a revolutionary who puts a fresh fire for taking territory back in the bones of the church. Tom is gifted to understand the relationships and the dynamics, which triggers a cultural shift. In this book, he explains revelatory truth, but more importantly, he imparts an apostolic strategy for taking cities, regions, and nations. I am glad he is on our side. Dr. Tom Schlueter sounds a clear apostolic call to embrace change in his book *Tribunals, The Authority of the Ekklesia to Legislate*. Change in the way we approach prayer. Change in the way we engage society. Change in the way we understand partnering with God. Change in the way we build our worldview. Throughout his book, Tom commissions us to make Earth like heaven. You will receive an impartation of supernatural faith, revolutionary instruction, and courage as you journey through the pages of this work and become part of the kingdom's mandate to transform society.

Bringing the kingdom of God in the way God intended for His Sons and Daughters to do! Throughout the world, God's people are fine-tuning their understanding of Jesus' mandate to disciple cities, regions, and nations. A passion is rapidly arising for pursuing aggressive, intentional social transformation through Kingdom efforts. Apostle Tom has been hearing what Holy Spirit is saying to the church. His brilliant new book, strong on experience and intense on practice, is what we all need to begin taking giant steps toward God's ultimate destiny for the world. You have not picked up this book by accident. You haven't wandered here by accident. There is a strategy to your journey and your assignment. A solution may be at hand. In the pages of this fantastic book, *Tribunals, The Authority of the Ekklesia to Legislate*, you may find what you need to fulfill your assignment as a mighty Kingdom advancer. I am honored to endorse this much-needed manuscript. Don't just read this work. Study it! Embrace it! Practice it! Luke 12:32 "Do not be afraid, little flock, for your Father has chosen gladly to give you the kingdom." (NASB)

Dr. Greg Hood, Th.D.
President, Kingdom University
Apostolic Leader at The Network of Five-Fold Ministers & Churches and
Kingdom Life Ekklesia,
Franklin, Tennessee
Author of: *The Gospel of the Kingdom*
Rebuilding The Broken Altar – Awaking Out of Chaos
Sonship According to the Kingdom
www.GregHood.org

Tribunals waves Heaven's flag of Victory in Christ! Allowing Abba to parent you through intimacy, discipline and love creates Jesus' reality of His Ekklesia! This writing is crafted for you to walk in the empowerment of Abba's original intent; a child of God, a way maker, a Bride to be presented to King Jesus our waiting Groom! The craftsmanship of Holy Spirit within you desires to finish you in Abba's Glory! Your family, community, state, and nation are desperate for His Glory! Well done, Abba. It also is not for religious, church followers! In fact, True Justice will destroy you! So..., maybe you should dive into *Tribunals* for your perfect destruction and a True raising from the dead. Better yet, *Tribunals* is so weighty with Truth that attempting to consume it without Holy Spirit will only cause you to "throw-up" with judgement, contempt and even jealousy. Caution is vital when considering *Tribunals*, mainly because an awakening lies hidden within Abba's intent for your life! Remember, the Veil was ripped in to for you! The Way, The Truth and The Life has a final comment to each of us, "let Abba parent you!" Well done, Tom.

Hollis Kirkpatrick
Servants to the City
TXAPN Coordinator, Rolling Plains Region

This book can be summed up in one word: JOY! Having known Dr. Tom Schlueter for 25 years and read his other books, I wondered how he would present both the practical aspects and the efficacy of *Tribunals*. I was blessed by the logical, point-by-point way he highlighted how God has led the Ekklesia into ever-deepening levels of prayer and intercession. In this book, are keys that open doors to opportunity and victorious results using *Tribunals*. I finished this book with absolute joy. This is a "now" book that you will want to digest and experience for yourself.

RaJean Thayer Vawter, President
Vawtermark Ministries, Inc.
TXAPN East Gate Co-coordinator

For four years, leaders from among the Ekklesia in our area, have been meeting monthly to worship, seek the Lord, listen, and decree those things which we hear Him saying for the 24-county, TXAPN East Gate region of Northeast Texas. As coordinators in the region, my wife and I were there the day that Tom first visited over three years ago and had his "this is that" moment concerning "tribunals." And, as they say, the rest is history. Tom's book chronicles much of what we've experienced in our growth as a regional tribunal. I highly recommend *Tribunals*. Among other things, it provides practical guidelines for a new wineskin within the Ekklesia that can positively impact regional transformation.

Gary E. Vawter
Vice-president, Vawtermark Ministries, Inc.
TXAPN East Gate Region Coordinator

Tribunals! Tom has done an excellent job in defining and explaining their purpose and Biblical context. Tom's humility, teaching gifts, and practical insight in this book will ignite the faith for many to begin this journey for their community, state, or nation. As a part of Kingdom University and the Indiana tribunals, I have experienced firsthand the gifts that Tom brings, his teaching, and Holy Spirit leading us to decree a thing that has brought forth mountain moving breakthrough. Only God can orchestrate the people, the timing, and the places -- only God could lead Tom to write this book for such a time as this!

Tammy Powers, PhD
Christian Counselor
Psalm 139 Counseling Services
Freedom & Fire Church, Co-Minister
Dean, College of Counseling, Kingdom University

Tribunals

I want to honor the faithful intercessors and other front-liners
who have worked diligently to see the purposes of Christ
accomplished in America.
Most of you are never paid a penny for your labors,
never receive glowing introductions,
and will never stand on a stage.
You're the nameless, faceless heroes
the prophets assured us were coming.
Thank God you're here. Your best days are ahead of you.
(Dutch Sheets)

Tribunals

The Authority of the Ekklesia to Legislate

Dr. Thomas Schlueter

© 2023 Thomas Schlueter
This book is protected by the copyright laws of the United States of America. This book may not be copied or reprinted for commercial gain or profit. The use of short quotations or occasional page copying for personal, or group study is encouraged. Permission will be granted upon request from Tom Schlueter. All rights reserved.

Any emphasis added to Scripture quotations is the author's own. Unless otherwise noted, Scripture quotations are taken from the New American Standard Bible, © 1960, 1962, 1963, 1968, 1971, 1972, 1973, 1975, 1977, 1995 by the Lockman Foundation," and The Passion Translation: New Testament with Psalms, Proverbs and Song of Songs, © 2020 by BroadStreet Publishing.

ISBN: 9798390168271
Imprint: Independently published

Dedication

I dedicate this book to my father, Arnold Schlueter. My dad passed away two years ago (February 23, 2021) after he had faithfully served the Lord for over seventy-five years as an ordained minister of the church. He had also been married for seventy-five years to my mom, Helen Schlueter.

Dad was always the one who encouraged me to go the distance with the Lord. He was the one, after many conversations regarding the future of the church, that would say, "We need to make sure that we were following the counsel of the Lord for the future of the church. It belongs to Him and He will build it." I remember one time when he came to visit us at our church in Arlington. We were sitting in a prayer room there in the building. He was a Spirit-filled preacher of the Lord. He was Lutheran, as was I. And his comment to me that morning somewhat caught me off guard. He looked over at me and took my hand and he declared, "Tom, you are a prophet of the Lord to this nation."

Thank you, Dad, for always standing there with me.

I also want to dedicate this book to Evangelist Steve Hill. Steve is now with the Lord but in the Spring of 2008, I was attending a gathering at his church in Dallas-Fort Worth. At the end of the meeting, he asked to talk with me. He invited me to come to his office the following Monday. I was surprised by the invitation because I had never had a one on one conversation with him. He was a powerful instrument of revival, which I personally witnessed, in Pensacola, Florida. We met in his office and talked for over an hour. At the end of our time, he pulled his chair in front of me and took my hands. He prophesied and prayed over me that I would be used as an instrument in the coming revival and awakening. I believe his words, and I believe this book is part of the trigger for that to happen.

Thank you, Steve.

Acknowledgements

I first and foremost want to acknowledge my beautiful bride, Kay. Later this year we will be celebrating forty-nine years of marriage. She has been the one who has faithfully stood by my side through thick and thin. She's been there when we've had great success and when I've pulled some "dunderhead things." She's the love of my life. She is my co-laborer with the Texas Apostolic Prayer Network. She is the resource person that helps sustain this ministry through all her creative products and ideas that she uses on her product tables. I love you, Honey. And I'm looking forward to many, many more years.

I wish to acknowledge Chuck Pierce, Dutch Sheets, Greg Hood, Clay Nash, Jim Hodges, Cindy Jacobs, Jacquie Tyre, and Regina Shank, who exemplify the meaning of apostolic and prophetic leadership and mentorship. They have been my most ardent supporters. They have been my strongest allies and encouragers. I thank the Lord that I am in covenant with them.

I acknowledge the most wonderful TXAPN leadership team: Lonnie and Rhonda Brooks, Penny Simmons, Ollie and Phyllis Wilburn, Kyle and Melisa Hooper, Mark Wauahdooah, Eddie and Merrie Cardin, Laura Mallory, Bud and Shirley Schmidt, Hollis and Carol Jean Kirkpatrick, Anne Tate, Jorge Lorenzana, Connie Swain, Peggy Connett, Laura Terrell, Wayne and Joyce Shaver, Dianne Young, Linda Dennis, Kristy Edwards, Linda Edwards, Trayce Bradford, Donna Craig, Diane Kirkwood, Gary and RaJean Vawter, Carmen Johnson, Gina Castro, Kirvin and Beckie Griffin, Pat Palmer, Donna Kelly, Jimmy and Martha Dusek, Fritz and Debra Rosenthal, Kat Rowoldt, Michael and Christy Maris, Gilda Wilkinson, Kim Ulmer, Patsy Chmelar, Kim Johnson, Cody and Cheri Clemmons, Robin Durham, Betty Johnson, Jason and April Blanchard, Nancy Nicholson, Bob Long, Nicole Smith, Cody and Rene'e Haynes, Neal and Darla Ryden, Gloria Wiggins, Wayne and Pam Stolz, Ken and Ginny Bryan, Tere Shipman, Debbie Bowman, Betty Huff, Amanda Rossy, Sharon Denney, Theresa Estrada, Jeremy and Tandy Burk, Emma Trimble, Wanda Ulrey, Linda Goodwin, Laura Reeves, Loretta Brown, Judy Torres, Gary and

Patricia Wilhite, Esther Gallegos, Frank and Ruby Dodson, Bev Hill, Dorothy and Chris Dundas, and Diana Longwell.

I acknowledge the wonderful Ekklesia that meets at Prince of Peace House of Prayer and how they have faithfully marched into their destiny and calling in God's Kingdom.

They worship through a God-ordained portal. They are family. Thank you, Kelly Wilson, for being a faithful servant and friend in the house and with TXAPN.

I want to acknowledge with great joy the women and men that make up War Room prayers. These saints meet every Wednesday with me. They carry out the truest meaning of a tribunal as they declare God's purposes into the atmosphere. Thank you, Christine Griggs, Kelly Wilson, Betty King, Darenda Anastazi, Angel Johnson, Janet Rae Askins, Susan Bautista, Lisa Brink, Phyllis Crawford, Christy Dunwoody, Linda Edwards, Perla Guzman, Suzanne Harrington, Patricia Hindman, Mikki Hunt, Carolyn Hurst, Patti Pace, Cindy Jackson, JoBeth Kested, Suzan Lupton, Vashti Mann, Ruth Potts, Teresa Roden, Tim Tremaine, Rocky Gathright, and Donita Satterwhite.

I cannot express with words the covenantal love I share with the Elders at the Gate: Jon Bunn, Burton Purvis, Hollis Kirkpatrick, Sam Dewald, Gregory Sherwood, Lewis Hogan, Michael Brennan, Chris Shields, and Jorge Lorenzana. And thank you David Munoz for the beautiful and powerful cover!

Table of Contents

Foreword		17
Introduction		21
Chapter One	Authority: We Need to Go to the Source	25
Chapter Two	Heaven Issues Our Passport	35
Chapter Three	How Are We To Pray?	43
Chapter Four	Tribunals: Part 1	51
Chapter Five	Tribunals: Part 2	61
Chapter Six	Don't Listen to the Forever Loser	87
Epilogue		91

Forewords

Tribunals are the way judgments were decreed throughout the Word of God, though this word is rarely understood in our modern-day life. However, the same results can be attained if we, as God's people, embrace the action and call today. Tom Schlueter has not only embraced this concept but leads teams in the spiritual practice of this incredible earth action which displays the authority of heaven on earth. What Tom shares in *Tribunals: The Authority of the Ekklesia to Legislate* not only develops a necessary concept but encourages us to realign heaven's purposes into the earth realm.

In this book, Tom gives us a new example of restoring the authority of God in the earth today. He is one of those incredible covenant people that God has in His Kingdom this hour to hold tribunals throughout America. Faith and authority must walk together to accomplish God's purposes.

Our most common understanding of a tribunal would be a judge sitting on a raised bench with a gavel and presiding from that position. The court then rules following presentation of the case before them. Before the Lord was crucified, Pilate addressed the crowd from his judgment seat (Matt. 27:19; John 19:13). Of course, the crowd chose wrongly ... after the presentation, they freed Barabbas and condemned Jesus. In this book, Tom has great examples of going to places to reverse wrong judgments previously made by an authority and the people of the tribunal's choice.

A tribunal is really important to understand as the ekklesia exercises authority in this new historical era of Kingdom rule. The public platform is important and is where civil cases were heard in the Roman Empire. Tribunal was often a designation for the court official who pronounced the judgment on the public platform. When the Corinthian Jews accused Paul before Gallio, they brought him before the bench. When Paul appeared before Festus at Caesarea, Festus was seated upon the bench (Acts 25:6, 17). Paul refers to this as the *"bench"* of Caesar (Acts 25:10), suggesting that this was the official judicial bench at Caesarea where the Roman governor resided and functioned. The term has a spiritual significance in Rom. 14:10 ("judgment seat of God") and 2 Cor. 5:10 ("judgment seat of Christ"). Both passages refer to the appearance of all people (including Christians) before God (or Christ) to be judged.

We are moving from a church era to a kingdom era. In this divine shift, the Lord is transforming our mindset, so we move outwardly from what has been built in one season into a fresh movement for the next. This will be a new time of building, but we must first unlock God's kingdom plan and align heaven and earth. When the Lord revealed His Messiahship to His disciples in Matthew 16, He gave Peter a prophetic word that would transcend the ages. In Matthew 16:18–19 (my paraphrase), He prophesied, "I will build My church, the gates of hell will not overpower it, and you will have authority to unlock the kingdom and forbid and permit what goes on in earth." We must remember that this prophecy to Peter had yet to be fully revealed in reality. *The church was still a mystery.* Therefore, when the day of Pentecost came, and three thousand were converted, Peter must have thought, "How will we build for the future? How will the Lord, who has ascended, accomplish this through us?"

The disciples did not have a full concept of the meaning of the "church." The only concept they had of a spiritual gathering was from the synagogue. The word used here is *ekklesia*, which was a Roman concept of ambassadors going in to transform a region and make it look like Rome. Everything seemed new to the disciples. Just a few weeks prior, they had a revelation of the Lord being Messiah. Now they had to see how to gather and build for the future out of a new paradigm. Eventually, they would have to leave Jerusalem to do this and build in Antioch a prototype of what the Lord was prophesying. The writer of Hebrews gave us much revelation of on what the Spirit of God was doing in that day that could not be done in Jerusalem. This is an example of how God built in one season—in this instance, how the church grew in Jerusalem and Judea—in order to move His church into a *new* season—and then to Antioch (modern-day southern Turkey) and to the uttermost ends of the earth.

This would begin a whole new era in the genesis of the early church. Now, the *Spirit of God* would help His leadership establish something that would be indestructible. There would be unsurpassed power in the ekklesia to overcome the enemy of mankind, Satan. But before the church was built, there had to be an unlocking of God's kingdom power within the triumphant people who would walk into the future. That is what the Book of Acts (in general) and Acts 2 (specifically) is about: the church was imbued with the power and purposes of the Holy Spirit.

We are living in a Passover Era. If we keep passing over and restoring the ancient understanding that God intended us to operate within, we will regain our vision. Without a vision, a people perish. In Proverbs 29:18, this word actually means that without boundaries or prophetic utterance, a people go backward. This is a critical point: We must remember that it took approximately seventy years to establish the first church expression. In every era, we unlock a kingdom plan so we can build the prototype for the ekklesia for the future. This new era propels us into a season of unlocking so that we can build in days ahead. That is exactly what God is doing—*right now*. He is "passing over" His people, looking for His church—that body of believers who will be used in this *pey* decade of harvest in the midst of world turmoil. While this entire *pey* decade is strategic, there is a seven-year period—late fall 2019 through 2026—that will *be most critical*. During these seven years, we will see a great rearrangement of economic power structures as well as spiritual power shifts. Watch. Pray. And when God releases you in your particular sphere and authority, move forward in boldness, not backward in fear.

Tom Schlueter is an excellent example of a leader whom God is using to help in His ultimate divine restoration. *Tribunals: The Authority of the Ekklesia to Legislate* is a great model for exercising God's restorative plan on earth.

Dr. Chuck D. Pierce
President of Glory of Zion International, Kingdom Harvest Alliance, and Global Spheres Inc.

It is my privilege and honor to write a foreword for Apostle Tom Schlueter's latest book, Tribunals. As many of you know, the revelation and understanding of the Church as a governing body, i.e., Ekklesia, is growing among the people of God globally. This is changing everything in the Church and in the world! The people of God are seeing themselves as more than a congregation. They now understand they are a Kingdom Congress vested with delegated authority and power to release the government of King Jesus into all spheres of life here on earth! They now understand why Jesus taught His disciples to pray: "Your Kingdom come, your will be done on earth as it is in heaven."

In this inspiring and informative book Tom tells the exciting story of the birth and emergence of the Texas Apostolic Prayer Network. Within the story, you will discover how the corporate Ekklesia functions on many levels: (1) the local church; (2) the state you live in; (3) the nation; and (4) the earth. The Biblical and theological truths shared in this volume will shift the Ekklesia to a new level of efficiency and impact. The term, 'tribunals' drives home the essential and most basic truths of the cross of Jesus! His cross is primarily about divine love and divine justice. Jesus covenantally, legislatively, and judicially defeated Satan and his evil powers. Based on Christ's victory, the Ekklesia Church He is building is the instrument on earth to implement His victory in history!

To say it another way, the Ekklesia, as a Kingdom Congress, is the means whereby the earth is reharmonized to heaven as the kingdoms of this world become the Kingdom of God and His Messiah. I must say that Tom's book is a manual where revelation leads to application. This is vitally important as we move forward in our callings and anointings. You will walk away from reading this book and know how to practically apply the deep truths found in it. Thanks, Tom, for blessing, inspiring, instructing, and challenging us!

Jim Hodges
Founder and President
Federation of Ministers and Churches International

Introduction

On June 7, 2007, over three hundred Texans gathered in the auditorium located inside the Texas State Capital in Austin. Something new was going to be birthed in the state of Texas. Apostle and Prophet Chuck Pierce had invited me (Tom Schlueter) a couple of months earlier to lead the movement of prayer and intercession in the State of Texas. My answer was "yes." Since that time, I have made it a point to connect and align with Chuck and other apostolic leaders in the state and nation to seek counsel, confirmation, or direction that they felt was essential regarding Texas and its future.

This covenantal alignment is essential in this new era where we are witnessing the apostolic and prophetic arising within the Ekklesia. This is not the old paradigm of an apostle "covering" a network of people but a season when the apostle, as a servant, father and leader, mentors, and trains up the grassroot Ekklesia in a state or nation.

I had come to one of those moments in 2019 and was seeking an opportunity to visit with Chuck at the Global Spheres Center in Corinth, Texas. The year has been an exceptionally busy one of traveling for him and so it was very difficult to find a time, but then his assistant, Brian, called me and told me that Chuck could meet with me later that week in August. He asked, "Are you available?" I did not hesitate in answering "yes."

When I finally was able to meet with Chuck along with my wife, one of the first things, he asked me was, "Tom, what do you sense is going on in the state of Texas?" I answered him that I was not sure what the full meaning was of the word that the Lord had been putting into my spirit, but that it was time to release "legislative groups" throughout the state of Texas. He immediately responded with excitement, and said, "that's it."

Sometimes we laugh about the process that followed but I asked Chuck what he thought it meant and his answer was again simple. "The Lord will continue to reveal that to you." And that is what is happening with all of us. God will continue to reveal His plans to us, and each of us need to have our spirits attentive to His voice as He directs us in whatever form of ministry we are involved with.

I was more than ready to receive from the Lord whatever revelation that He needed to give me regarding these legislative groups. But as we always do, we continued to do what the Lord had already told us to do. We travel the land. We meet with the leaders or coordinators of the council. We carry out the assignments that He's given us to do. We simply proceed in obedience.

One of those journeys took us to Laredo, Texas, where we met with council members from the Valley, Coastal Bend, Plateau, and Mission Regions of our network. I started sharing about the revelation the Lord had given me regarding the legislative groups. We went into prayer and began to discuss what this might be about. My wife Kay spoke up and said that the word the Lord was giving her was "tribunal." Some of us knew what the word meant, because it identifies a court that is usually held in the military, but as we continued to research it using that great resource, Google, we discovered that this was exactly what the Lord wanted to birth in the state. Kay made it clear that even though we typically would think of it in terms of a military court, she was also seeing it as the gathering of the chiefs of Native American tribes coming together as a council to make the decisions regarding the tribe.

One online dictionary rendered this definition: **"a court of justice or any place where justice is administered."** Words related to tribunal included court of law, committee, judge, justice, bar, bench, council, forum, magistrate, and judiciary. We will define tribunal in more detail later, but it was obvious that the Lord wanted us to embrace this revelation.

This is interesting because the word for church that is used in the New Testament is Ekklesia, and it represents a governmental aspect of the church that many times we have left covered up by our religious practices. He wants the Ekklesia to be an influential part of His kingdom, which is meant to literally transform, shift, and legislate His kingdom in the earth as it has been expressed from heaven. The tribunal fits perfectly with this notion because it represents the idea of a court, a congress, or a council getting together to determine what the Lord would like to have determined and then decreed on earth. It becomes a place where we can legislate out of His kingdom principles. What is it that He needs released into our cities, communities, states, and nation? We were excited to find out. We were excited to see it develop.

But then the Covid pandemic hit the nation. Everything locked down. Suddenly, our trips came to an end. We were told to stay put. We were told to mask up. We were even told as churches to lock down. And many did. Prince of Peace House of Prayer in Arlington, Texas, and Texas Apostolic Prayer Network (TXAPN) did not. The first Sunday of lockdowns, I did broadcast the worship service from my church office. There were ten people that joined us at the table. The next weekend was the weekend when we celebrated the Passover Seder. It was a powerful demonstration of Passover as we made sure that everyone was carrying out a Seder celebration in their own homes with their families around their own tables. It was a powerful time, and we knew that something new was on the other side of Passover.

People were not leaving their homes though. Kay and I we're getting a little stir crazy. We were making small trips every day just to get ice cream or whatever else, but we finally decided it was time for us to get back on the road. We decided to drive to Tyler, Texas. We had heard that our good friends, Kerry and Diane Kirkwood and Gary and RaJean Vawter were having prayer gatherings at the Reformation House of Prayer in Tyler, and we decided to join them on a Thursday morning. We drove the two hours to Tyler and arrived just as they started at 10 o'clock in the morning. We walked into a room that was filled with forty or more people. None of them were wearing masks, and they were filled with joy. In the room, there was a representation of at least twelve to fourteen of the counties which make up our East Gate Region of TXAPN. They started with worship, then announced a purposed goal for prayer for the morning. They took a rollcall of the counties that were present, and then they began to make decrees and declarations as they legislated into the East Gate and into the counties that made it up.[1]

The Lord spoke to my heart and said, "This is it. This is the Tribunal."

In the following chapters, we will lay out what the Lord has revealed since then, regarding the development of the Tribunals or these legislative councils. But we need to take you on a journey. We need to understand that there is a foundation or a source from which all this flows. We cannot just jump into doing something new and hoping that it will be carried out like old strategies of times past that were based on religious mindsets. We are in a new place, and we must listen carefully to how the Lord is developing His Ekklesia in this hour.

---

[1] Diane Kirkwood gives a testimony of this in Chapter 5

1

Authority: We Need to Go To The Source

*And I will make enemies
Of you and the woman,
And of your offspring and her Descendant;
He shall bruise you on the head,
And you shall bruise Him on the heel." (Genesis 1:15)*

But the court will convene for judgment, and his dominion will be taken away, annihilated and destroyed forever. Then the sovereignty, the dominion, and the greatness of all the kingdoms under the whole heaven will be given to the people of the saints of the Highest One; His kingdom will be an everlasting kingdom, and all the empires will serve and obey Him.' (Daniel 7:26-27)

I will give you the keys of the kingdom of heaven; and whatever you bind on earth shall have been bound in heaven, and whatever you loose on earth shall have been loosed in heaven." Then He gave the disciples strict orders that they were to tell no one that He was the Christ. (Matthew 16:19-20)

Kingdom Authority[2]

(Portions of this chapter are borrowed from my book Return of the Priests.)

Let me begin by reviewing the definition of priesthood the Lord gave me in 2004.

The priesthood is a call initiated, defined, and

---

[2] Return of the Priests: Discovering God's True Intent for His People by Thomas Schlueter

empowered by God. The priesthood is an invitation based on our covenant relationship of faith into an intimate fellowship with God. The priesthood is carried out – not in the framework of a religious system – but in everyday lives. The priesthood includes all people called, claimed, and redeemed by God's sovereign will and grace through Jesus Christ. The priesthood is expressed through our lives by an authority we are given by God to serve in His kingdom in response to that intimate relationship with Him. God has called us to priesthood. Priesthood is not something that we define. It's not empowered by us. God is the One who has anointed or crowned us for this work.

What the Lord has released in my heart is that we, as individuals and as a church body (the Ekklesia), are to be in alignment with God's rule, which is His kingdom. The way that we come into alignment with God's rule is through intimate fellowship with Him. Everything is in His hands. He is the ruler. He is the One Who reigns. God is the One who ordains our steps.

God makes this extremely clear in Psalm 24:1-2:

> *The earth is the LORD's, and all it contains,*
> *The world, and those who dwell in it.*
> *For He has founded it upon the seas*
> *And established it upon the rivers.*

Years ago, a professor of mine had us look at the Apostles' Creed which begins with the confession: "I believe in God the Father Almighty, Creator of Heaven and Earth." He then said: "We need to read this differently." We should confess: "I believe in God the Father Almighty, Creator, Owner, and Ruler of Heaven and Earth." Then…

> *…God said, "Let Us make man in Our image, according to Our likeness; and let them rule over the fish of the sea and over the birds of the sky and over the cattle and over all the earth, and over every creeping thing that creeps on the earth." 27 God created man in His own image, in the image of God He created him; male and female He created them. 28 God blessed them; and God said to them, "Be fruitful and multiply, and fill the earth, and subdue it; and rule over the fish of the sea and over the birds of the sky and over every living thing that moves on the earth." (Genesis 1:26-28)*

He made us to be the expressions of His rule on earth. He never gave up ownership or ultimate rule or reign over all of creation. But His desire, plan and original design was that we would now be those that represent or carry out that rule and authority on earth as it is in heaven. As I often declare to people when I need to tell them that they are now the ones responsible, the Lord has also said to us: "Tag, you're it." But something wrong happened.

In the above passage from Genesis 1:15, it declares that the woman's seed would crush or bruise the head of the serpent's descendants. Adam and Eve had rebelled against God's plan. They were deceptively drawn into Satan's plan to wrest away authority from humanity and to take it for himself. This brought about God's judgment upon Adam and Eve. But even during the judgment, God decrees a promise of what will take place in the future.

The word for bruise (Strong's H7779[3]) in Hebrew means to crush, seize, or fall upon his head. The word head refers to the natural head of the serpent but speaks more importantly of his headship or his authority. In other words, Jesus will eventually take back the headship or authority that Satan received when we rebelled in the garden. And once again, He will deliver it to us – the Ekklesia.

So, our role as priests includes this kingship or headship mandate to rule over Satan and his attempts to retrieve authority.

Here is the key: We need to position ourselves, as priests, to hear God's voice – to be aligned with His heart – and to bring forth His kingdom as we journey through our lives. God is ordering our steps. Either we believe that, or we don't believe it. It's that simple. God is ordering our steps. That doesn't give us permission to lean back and say, "God, go on and do it. I don't even have to participate." No, God is looking for an intimate, participating relationship with us as priests and kings, and in that participation with Him, He releases us and directs us into where we need to be going. He empowers the reign and authority of His kingdom through our obedience. This task includes all of us. It is not in any way or fashion limited to the traditional leaders or committees of the church to carry out these assignments. Late last year (2022), I was doing my early morning devotions in the front room of our house. I was looking out the large picture window. The Lord spoke to me and asked me, "have you considered the blade of grass?" He usually speaks to me in very simple phrases or questions. I waited for Him to answer the question. He revealed to me that a grassroots movement is totally dependent on every blade of grass. No one, of His called out people, is left out.

This ordering of our steps is all a part of that definition of a priest. We are called. God defines the call. God empowers our priesthood. The priesthood is for our everyday

---

[3] Strong, James. The New Strong's Exhaustive Concordance of the Bible, Nashville, TN: Thomas Nelson Publishers, 1990.

lives. It is not just a religious order that has been defined by the church for so many centuries. The priesthood was always meant to be for the everyday people.

Releasing God's Expression

God's authority and His dominion through us into the world is what priesthood is all about. Let this sink in. We are dealing here with a major paradigm shift. This is a major changing of our thoughts. One of the worst deceptions that the enemy has used on the people of God is that when you begin to talk about priesthood, then you must be talking about fulltime ministry. And if you are talking about fulltime ministry, you must make plans for seminary or Bible college. But fulltime ministry is not tied, in God's eyes, with seminary or Bible college. Ouch! Did I really say that? A seminary or Bible college is a tool used by God for the training up of certain giftings but is not a necessary tool for fulltime ministry. This is where the major paradigm shift takes place. Every single one of you is in fulltime ministry as priests and kings.

I've been in ministry as a pastor for almost 45 years, and there was always one question that seemed to come to the top when members of the congregation would come to visit with me. They would often ask or comment, "I'm not sure what my call is?" After conversing with them, I knew what they were asking. They wanted to know what kind of occupation they needed to be doing. I always wished that I had had a little black book in my pocket that listed all their names and the jobs that they were supposed to have, but that was not happening. I struggled with these conversations because I didn't know what jobs they should have. I could give them some suggestions or ideas based on the conversation that we were having, but I really didn't know. As I asked the Lord about this many times, He finally answered me and said, "Their call is simple. They are kings and priests who represent My Kingdom?" He then went on to share a very surprising answer. "I could care less what their occupation is." Now, if the Lord could speak tongue in cheek, I believe that's what He was doing. I do believe He cares about our occupations, but regardless of what occupation we were in, our call would always be the same. You are a king and a priest of God Most High.

God wants to release that truth into our lives and then release it through us to others. The Lord is restoring this truth to His Church.

Releasing the Kingdom

Now, let's concentrate on the last portion of the definition of priesthood. Let's look at it in several parts: There is already an assumption that you are a priest, and that the priesthood is expressed through your life. Now the question is – how is that accomplished? We are given an authority by God to serve His kingdom and to release His kingdom or His reign into the world in response to our intimate relationship with Him.

In June of 2003, I attended a time of strategic prayer in Washington D.C. Our prayers were focused on the Supreme Court of the United States. I was so excited during those prayers when Dutch Sheets shared this word from the Lord.

"You will fully shift the government of America when you shift the prayer movement from priestly intercession only to kingly intercession."

Priestly intercession is primarily focused on worship and petition, whereas kingly intercession releases God's reign and authority into the world. In Revelation 8:6-10, we see this truth demonstrated.

And I saw between the throne (with the four living creatures) and the elders a Lamb standing, as if slain, having seven horns and seven eyes, which are the seven Spirits of God, sent out into all the earth. And He came and took the book out of the right hand of Him who sat on the throne. When He had taken the book, the four living creatures and the twenty-four elders fell down before the Lamb, each one holding a harp and golden bowls full of incense, which are the prayers of the saints. And they sang a new song, saying, "Worthy are You to take the book and to break its seals; for You were slain and purchased for God with Your blood men from every tribe and tongue and people and nation. **"You have made them to be a kingdom and priests to our God; and they will reign upon the earth."** *(emphasis added)*

As the prayers of the saints (priests) ascend to heaven, they are received by the Father; and in response, He releases His power through them on the earth.

When we worship God as priests, He releases us as kings.

God's goal is to be worshipped, not just for the sake of being worshipped, but so that all the nations of the world may be delivered to Him. And the peoples of the earth are delivered to God when His priests act upon the kingdom authority granted to them.

What is Kingdom Authority?

Let's consider this authority that God is releasing to us as priests. "Kingdom authority" is granted to us as priests. What does that mean? Turn to Isaiah 61. Read the first six verses.

The Spirit of the Lord GOD is upon me,
Because the LORD has anointed me
To bring good news to the afflicted;
He has sent me to bind up the brokenhearted,
To proclaim liberty to captives
And freedom to prisoners;
To proclaim the favorable year of the LORD
And the day of vengeance of our God;
To comfort all who mourn,
To grant those who mourn in Zion,
Giving them a garland instead of ashes,
The oil of gladness instead of mourning,
The mantle of praise instead of a spirit of fainting.
So they will be called oaks of righteousness,
The planting of the LORD, that He may be glorified.
Then they will rebuild the ancient ruins,
They will raise up the former devastations;
And they will repair the ruined cities,
The desolations of many generations.
Strangers will stand and pasture your flocks,
And [e]foreigners will be your farmers and your vinedressers.
But you will be called the priests of the LORD;
You will be spoken of as ministers of our God.
You will eat the wealth of nations,
And in their riches you will boast.

As you read it, you should have realized that this passage is referring to the coming Messiah – Jesus. We know that Jesus used these very words when He spoke at the synagogue in Nazareth (Luke 4:18-19). Jesus said, "Today this Scripture is fulfilled in your hearing (Luke 4: 21b)." We know that the prophet Isaiah was prophesying about Jesus, the Messiah, and His anointed work.

Now, understand this clearly. You are in Christ, and Christ is in you. Whatever anointing, whatever empowering, whatever calling came upon Jesus, the Son of God, has been ultimately released also into you. So, everything about this passage, as it speaks about Jesus, also speaks about you – individually and corporately.

Let's see what the Lord is saying about YOU. "The Spirit of the Lord God is upon me..." Yes! The Spirit of the Lord is upon YOU. "...because the Lord has anointed me (YOU)." What's very powerful about the word anointing is that refers to the process of rubbing oil upon one's head, but the purpose of that anointing was to demonstrate that this person is now crowned. Jesus was crowned as King over all. You have been crowned as a son and daughter of the Most High God. You have been crowned as a king and a priest.

> L ORD, our Lord,
> How majestic is Your name in all the earth,
> You who have displayed Your splendor above the heavens!
> From the mouths of infants and nursing babies You have established strength
> Because of Your enemies,
> To do away with the enemy and the revengeful.
> When I consider Your heavens, the work of Your fingers,
> The moon and the stars, which You have set in place;
> What is man that You think of him,
> And a son of man that You are concerned about him?
> Yet You have made him a little lower than God,
> **And You crown him with glory and majesty!**
> **You have him rule over the works of Your hands;**
> **You have put everything under his feet,**
> All sheep and oxen,
> And also the animals of the field,
> The birds of the sky, and the fish of the sea,
> Whatever passes through the paths of the seas.
> L ORD, our Lord, How majestic is Your name in all the earth!
> (Psalm 8 emphasis added))

This revelation goes back to the definition. God is the One Who initiates and empowers all of this. God has anointed you to do what? God has anointed you "to preach good tidings to the poor;" He has sent you "to heal the brokenhearted, to proclaim liberty to the captives, and the opening of the prison to those who are bound; to proclaim the acceptable year of the LORD and the day of vengeance of our God to comfort all who mourn, to console those who mourn in Zion, to give them beauty for ashes, the oil of joy for mourning, the garment of praise for the spirit of heaviness; that they may be called trees of righteousness, the planting of the LORD, that He may be glorified." Now look at what you are going to be involved in doing: "And they (you) shall rebuild the old ruins, they (you) shall raise up the former desolations, and they (you) shall repair the ruined cities, the desolations of many generations. Strangers shall stand and feed your flocks, and the sons of the foreigner shall be your plowmen and your vinedressers. But you shall be named the priests of the LORD. They shall call you the servants of our God.

You shall eat the riches of the Gentiles, and in their glory, you shall boast" (Isaiah 61:1-6 emphasis added).

This passage declares that we shall be named the priests of the Lord, and we shall be called His servants. When God's anointing, or crowning, comes upon us, as we spend time in relationship with Him, He releases kingdom authority in and through our lives. During a time of worship in one of our Tribunal meetings, we were singing the popular song Way Maker[4]. In the middle of the song, the Lord spoke clearly to me and declared, "This song is about you, too. You are way makers, miracle workers, promise keepers and light in the darkness. That's who you are!"

The Kingdom of God

There are many good books regarding the Kingdom of God that can give us a fuller understanding of the Kingdom of God. One of the best is The Gospel of the Kingdom by my friend Greg Hood but let me give you some defining statements of what the Kingdom of God is so we can understand a little more about what is being released in and through our lives.

- **God's Kingdom is a kingdom that will restore what was lost in Eden and throughout history.** What was lost? First and foremost – the intimate relationship intended between God and man. Secondly, we lost our intended destiny to live, work and reign as His children (the crown of His creation) on earth (Psalm 8). God sent His Son to save that which was lost (Matthew 18:11). God's kingdom, revealed through Jesus, restores that intimate relationship and our ability to have dominion as His children. As Greg says: "God was not interested in restoring religion."
- **God's Kingdom will be manifested (revealed or shown) as God's Glory extends over all the earth.** We are going to see God's glory and kingdom extend over all the earth. "Glory," according to Vine's Expository Dictionary means "honor; glory; great quantity; multitude; wealth; reputation [majesty]; splendor." "Kabod" refers to the "great physical weight or 'quantity' of a thing." Therefore, the basic definition of "God's glory" is the weight, power, and splendor of God. When we serve as kingly priests, God's glory, or the weight of His glory and authority, is released.
- **God's Kingdom will be defined as God's sovereign rule through Jesus Christ.** God's Kingdom is not defined by the size of churches, the size of ministries, or the influence of ministry. The Kingdom of God is not defined by personality. God's Kingdom is not defined by knowing the Bible backwards and forwards. The Kingdom of God will be here when God is sovereignly ruling through His

---

[4] Way Maker by Sinach (Osinachi Joseph) 2016

Son, Jesus Christ. The Kingdom of God is defined by God's sovereign rule. That sovereign rule is going to usher in the end of sin, death, and the power of Satan. God's sovereign rule is ushering in righteousness, holiness, salvation, hope, faith, and life.

- **God's Kingdom is a kingdom that is already in our midst, but not yet here.** We have a foretaste of God's Kingdom. Jesus announced that the "The Kingdom is here." It is **not coming later** in the "sweet by and by." It is here but it is still manifesting and growing in our midst. God's kingdom and His reign, or government, is ever increasing on the earth (Isaiah 9). It will continue to increase as we carry out our roles as kings and priests.
- **God's Kingdom is a kingdom that will come as a kingdom of priests cry out to God, "Your Kingdom come; Your will be done on earth as it is in Heaven!"** God is waiting for us to usher in the Kingdom of God. He's waiting for us to stand up as sons and daughters, and say, "Your Kingdom come; Your will be done on earth as it is in Heaven!" Declare it, saints! Speak it out, you priests! I entreat you. I beg you. Please declare the kingdom of God.
- **God's Kingdom is the Heart of the Gospel.** The Good News is the Kingdom of God. That news includes are participation in that kingdom as we confess our faith In Jesus Christ, but that confession is not just about getting a ticket to heaven. I don't want to oversimplify this, but one friend told me, "Our salvation prayer was but the coin toss in a game. Now it's time to win the game." It is about fully embracing who we are as kingdom people.
- **God's Kingdom transforms our world as God releases His reign over us.** He will begin to transform the place where we are positioned as His priests. God will begin to establish His reign in our location, but His reign or His Kingdom is not defined by location. God is waiting for a royal priesthood, a holy nation, a kingdom of priests to invite Him to rule over the entire earth.

2

Heaven Issues Our Passport

For our citizenship is in heaven, from which we also eagerly wait for a Savior, the Lord Jesus Christ, who will transform the body of our lowly condition into conformity with His glorious body, by the exertion of the power that He has even to subject all things to Himself. (Philippians 3:20-21)

Several years ago, I was on a mission trip. During that trip we needed to enter a country that is very dark and foreboding. As we entered the land, we checked in at the border security. They gathered all our passports. They told us that we would receive them back when we left the country. I had never had that happen to me before. And so, I was a little bit concerned. We proceeded to go into the country. We spent several hours there ministering to people and villages. On the way out we stopped at the Border Security Post. We went through very strict and thorough security and our passports were returned to us.

Our passport identifies our citizenship. My passport clearly states that I am a citizen of the United States of America. In that passport. I have many stamps that have recorded all the countries that I have been in over the last several decades. I am using my third passport since they expire every ten years and, the other two were filled with stamps.

The passport is my identity. Even though there was a period spanning several hours when I did not hold my United States passport in my hand, I still knew that I was a citizen of the United States, but I also knew that I had another passport. My United States passport declares that I am a citizen of this nation, but I also have another passport that is secured in heaven. It decrees that I am a citizen of heaven.

For our citizenship is in heaven, from which we also eagerly wait for a Savior, the Lord Jesus Christ; who will transform the body of our lowly condition into conformity with His glorious body, by the exertion of the power that He has even to subject all things to Himself.

(Philippians 3:20-21)

That passport supersedes all others. It identifies who I am. It identifies my purpose. It identifies my mission. It identifies who owns me and to whom I am loyal. That passport can never be overfilled. It never expires. It can never be rejected. I am sealed for eternity. I am a citizen of heaven. I am a son of the Most High God. My passport was issued to me by my Lord and Savior Jesus Christ when I committed my life to Him. And I declared that I would serve Him and represent Him throughout eternity.

When we go into another nation. We need to understand that we are representing our nation. But with this heavenly passport we represent our heavenly King. We are representing Him wherever we go and whatever we do. This passport is not limited to just our journeys into a foreign land. We are representing of the Heavenly King in every sphere of influence that we live in. We need to fully understand and embrace this one clear revelation about our citizenship in heaven: regardless of where we are and what we are doing we represent the Lord.

Dutch Sheets writes: "In yesterday's post, I spoke of representing Christ. A representative derives their authority from the person or entity they represent. The word means "to re-present" or "present again." A representative "presents again" the will and desires of the one who authorized them, speaking and acting on their behalf. In legal terms, this would be like a "power of attorney." This is the arrangement Christ has established with the church. We have personal authority to implement our will and desires, of course, but to operate in Christ's authority - in His name - we must be implementing His Word and will. As we do so, His authority and the power of Holy Spirit back up our efforts."[5]

Some Do Not

Many in the church have not grasped this truth. They have dedicated their lives to Jesus Christ. They have expressed their devotion to Him. They gather to serve Him and worship Him on Sunday mornings. But they have no concept of what it means to fully represent Him in the world in which they live. Please do not misunderstand me. Many Christians are doing good deeds on behalf of the Lord, but when we fully understand that we represent Him to the world, it means that we are releasing the full authority of heaven and the will of God – the Kingdom of God and His government – into the very structures of earth which we inhabit.

We are to be influencers in every realm of society. We are to be God's agents on the earth. We need to make sure that every aspect of life, where we have a sphere of influence, is moving towards an alignment with the kingdom and will of our Father in

---

[5] Dutch Sheets. GiveHim15. March 1, 2023

heaven. That includes education, government, the media, businesses, and our families. Everything that our lives touch can be and should be influenced by our role as citizens of heaven. For instance, regarding government, we should be praying diligently for God to bring godly leaders into positions of authority over our lives. But our participation must also include the process of voting, and yes. even possibly running for those offices. As citizens of heaven, we re-present Jesus and influence society with His will. Those in office need to embrace the truth that they are "ministers of the gospel."[6]

But some people do not properly represent the passport they hold. We can look at the world around us and we will readily recognize that people who are citizens of the United States are not always representing the United States in a way that honors our nation or upholds its principles. There are common people as well as leaders in government and education that are trying to dismantle the very Biblical core beliefs of who we are meant to be as a nation. They show no respect and in many ways are disgusted with the very nation that they claim as their own.

Our government is a constitutional republic. Our government is defined by our constitution and its strength lies **not** in a strong federal government but in the active representation of each citizen. When we don't properly represent our nation, we are literally handing our passport over to some foreign entity or belief system. Many people, claiming citizenship, are now granting loyalty to foreign systems like socialism, communism, or humanism. Many people have the sole desire of destroying the very core nature of who we are as a nation, and they have lost all understanding of the principles that our nation was built upon, which include the foundational truths of God's Holy Word.

But wait a minute! Are we talking about the passports that we hold as United States citizens or are we talking about the passports that we hold as citizens of heaven? We are talking about both. Over the last several decades the church has done the very same thing. We have abandoned our core beliefs. We have bought into the systems of the world. We have taken the opinion that we're going to hang in there until Jesus comes and we will let government, education and media determine the direction that our nation needs to go. We have abandoned the very core beliefs that are specified in other heavenly passports. When we do this, we have handed the passport of heaven

---

[6] Therefore, *you* must be subject, not only because of wrath but also for conscience' sake. For because of this you also pay taxes, for they are God's ministers attending continually to this very thing. Render therefore to all their due: taxes to whom taxes *are due*, customs to whom customs, fear to whom fear, honor to whom honor" (Romans 13:5-7 NKJV))

over to another group. By doing this we have dealt a deathly blow to our government, our educational systems, our arts, and entertainment industries and maybe most important of all – our families. We are allowing foreign entities (rulers, powers, the world forces of this darkness, and the spiritual forces of wickedness in the heavenly places) to have full access. To make matters worse, we have declared that we will do these things with our own wisdom and our own understanding, but we will fail miserably.

Let me share another story that helps us understand who owns us and how are lives are to reflect that ownership.

We Are Branded

> *"Behold, the days are coming," says the Lord, "when I will make a new covenant unlike the others that many have broke before. But this is the covenant, I will law my brand within them, I will write it in their hearts, and I will be their God, and they will be My people." (Jeremiah 31:31-34)*

The coordinators of the sixteen regions of the Texas Apostolic Prayer Network meet twice a year to worship, fellowship and strategize. One of the very significant revelations made at our mid-year gathering in January of 2023 was the "Espiritu de Jesus" branding iron.

Loretta Brown[7], one of our coordinators for the Coastal Bend Region of TXAPN writes:

"It's been said that the Father brings life, Jesus brings Dominion and Holy Spirit brings Honor. The Jesuit priests about 350 years ago gave the Queen of Spain a cattle brand to give to the Royal DeLeon Family as a gift to the New World. They migrated from Spain into the Spanish territory of Mexico, and later Martin DeLeon became an Empresario who settled on his land grant on the Gulf Coast of present-day Texas. His highest aspiration was to build a cathedral to honor God like those in Spain. This brand that looks like an E is an EDJ, Espiritu De Jesus – The Spirit of Jesus. This was the first brand registered before Texas was even established in 1807. Before Texas was even established, God saw it fit to **Brand Texas with the Spirit of Jesus**. The truth is, God marked His whole creation with His mark. I've warred over this brand for at least 20 years. The Lord has called me to cleanse and redeem time, land, generations, and birthrights. This brand represents years of redemption and setting Texas free to become a leader in the Nation to bring us back from

---

[7] Loretta is a seventh generation descendent of Martin DeLeon.

the brink of death. Red Stegall, a famous Cowboy poet, said it well: 'A man's brand is his own special mark. You can tell the measure of a man as to who he rides for. It's a sign of loyalty, honor, and respect. When you ride for a brand, you can count on that man covering your bets, but you ride for one that signs your check.' Jesus wrote the check of paying the ultimate price for us. Texas welcomes the Nation to join us in Riding for the Brand, Espiritu de Jesus."

Without going into all the details of the revelation that God has given us, it comes down to a very simple assignment and process. The Lord wants Texas branded with his Name – the Spirit of Jesus. We have discovered that this is not a moment to brand ministries or people or any old religious systems of the church. The Lord is redeeming the land and preparing it for its awakening and alignment with the Kingdom.

Chip Schweiger, The Cowboy Accountant, in his blog entitled "What It Means To Ride For The Brand," writes:

"In the old west cowboys lived by a code, the code of the west. This code was informal, unwritten, but well-understood by everyone who agreed to live the cowboy life on the open range. One of those unwritten rules, passed by mouth to ear from old cowboys to new ranch hands, was that the cowboy should always "ride for the brand." In the early days of the American west, a brand was a ranch's trademark, used to separate and document ownership of livestock. The brand also represented pride, duty, and stewardship, which inspired loyalty and dedication…. As to riding for a brand, cowboy poet Red Steagall summed it up best in one of his poems that earned him recognition as the Official Cowboy Poet of Texas, *"Son, a man's brand is his own special mark that says this is mine, leave it alone. You hire out to a man, ride for his brand, and protect it like it was your own."* So, what does it mean to ride for a brand? How do we know when and how to ride for a brand? In the old west, when a cowboy rode for the brand, it meant that he had signed on to the mission, goals and aims of the ranch owner. It meant that he was committed and that he was a dedicated team player. It meant, in the words of Red Steagall, that he gave his promise to protect the brand as though it were his own."[8]

Lana Vawser, a prophet from Australia, sent a word to me in April of 2017 (six years ago). It was for Texas. It confirms the Lord's desire to brand us. She wrote:

---

[8] Chip Schweiger, The Cowboy Accountant, in his blog entitled "What It Means To Ride For The Brand"

> I saw a BRANDING IRON on fire and the Lord was holding it, and He brought it down into the middle of Texas and placed it upon the ground and it burnt the word JESUS into the center of Texas. His name burnt SO BRIGHTLY and His name was seen from far and wide. His name was lifted high! A mighty move of My Spirit is upon you! I am coming with FIRE and My name shall be branded on the heart of Texas and My name and My fire, the fire of My presence and My love will spread far and wide. The greatest AWAKENING is upon Texas right now.[9]

So, whether it is a passport or a brand, Lord has set us aside, His Ekklesia, to release His Kingdom on Earth as it is in heaven. He has branded us. He has called us his own. He has issued us our heavenly passport. Let me finish this chapter by bringing an illustration of how important it is that we carry out this role. In our families., and every sphere of influence that surrounds us.

Eric Metaxas in his book <u>Letter to the American Church</u> shares the importance of standing up boldly for the nation that has issued our passport. President Ronald Reagan was headed to Germany to deliver a speech. He desired to forcefully express his opinion of the evil that was represented by the Soviet Union and the wall that separated West and East Berlin. His advisors, Chief of Staff Howard Baker and General Colin Powell were adamantly opposed to any statements that would only fuel the fire. Eric writes:

"Of course, one cannot help but suspect that establishment figures like Baker and Powell—like so many Republicans today, and so many in the American Church today—were in fact comfortable with the status quo. Often in history, leaders think of something as a "necessary evil" that cannot be vanquished and are only too happy to stand aside and let it continue, as though trying to bring it down is naïve and foolish. Most in Wilberforce's day thought of the slave trade this way. To go against such things was to tilt at windmills. But Reagan—like so many great leaders—was willing to come across as wild and unpredictable in how he led if that was necessary. He was certainly sickened by the fathomless evil of the Soviet Union and refused simply to see it as inevitable "status quo." He clearly wanted to do anything he could to bring down what just four years earlier he had infamously called "the Evil Empire," which was another example of what his critics saw as his impolitic approach. So, Reagan was not about to let those around him dissuade him from saying what he clearly felt must be said in West Berlin that day. The world would be watching. And so that day, he said it, and with steel in his voice delivered the now famous line – "Mr. Gorbachev, tear down this wall!" And when he said it, something happened. It was as though those words were more than words and carried tremendous spiritual power. Because when he spoke to them, a crack began to appear in what so many had thought of as an adamantine

---

[9] Lana Vawser: Texas - There is a Great Move of God Upon You, April 13, 2017

edifice. It was as though with the single deft and well-aimed blow of those words, the world changed. People suffering in Soviet prisons would hear about it and would tap about it through the walls to each other. Someone out there, far away from them, knew about them and was fighting for them. Someone out there cared enough to boldly speak against the evil that imprisoned them and millions of other fellow sufferers. Someone out there believed in truth and freedom and was not afraid to fight for these ideals. We can hardly imagine how much hope that one line delivered to prisoners around the world."[10]

"We would not have made it to the Coliseum." The Lord poured that revelation into my spirit as I was driving home from a prayer assignment in Austin. I knew immediately what He meant. Today's "religious" and "impassionate church" would not have been a threat to Nero or the Caesars that gathered the early saints into the Coliseum of Rome.

We must hold fast to our heavenly passport. For it grants us the authority and the kingdom access that the Lord desires for us to have in every realm of society.

---

[10] Letter to the American Church by Eric Metaxas

3

How Are We To Pray?

Our marvelous words are living miracles;
no wonder I long to obey everything you say.
Break open your Word within me until revelation-light shines out!
Those with open hearts are given insight into your plans.
I open my mouth and inhale the Word of God
because I crave the revelation of your commands.
(Psalm 119:129-131 The Passion Translation)

For many years now, the Lord has instructed me to encourage or exhort the Ekklesia to realize that every single member of the Ekklesia is an intercessor. I have oftentimes asked people in large groups to raise their hands if they are an intercessor. Out of a hundred people, there might be a dozen that raise their hands. I tell them: "Let's try that again." After a while, they realize that every single one of them needs to raise their hand. Why? Because the word intercession does not primarily relate to the role of prayer. It is a position of being a "go between" that each one of us has. I shared this thought in my book, Return of the Priests.

"God showed me that intercession is not a special gift or anointing. Intercession is a position. God desires that we intercede or pray for others in whatever place or position He has appointed for us. A woman, in her position as mother, will pray for her children. A man, in his position as father, will pray for his family. A person, in the position of employer, will pray for those who work at his or her company. People, in their position as citizens, will intercede for their city or nation. God showed me that Jesus was in the perfect position of intercession as He hung upon the cross. Jesus prayed from the cross, but it was not His prayers that saved us. It was His position of intercession between God and our sins that saved us from the judgment we deserve."[11]

Now let me clarify a portion of that quote that the Lord has released to me since I wrote it. I do believe that there are persons that have an anointing for intercessory prayer that takes them into special roles and positions of intercession. For example, every parent should be praying over their children, but there will be people who will go into travailing intercession over the children of the world as they witness them having to endure horrific lives. Each of us should be praying for legislators who represent us in the nation or the state, but there will be certain intercessors that will plant themselves in the halls of government to release God's authoritative prayers into those halls.

I believe that we've entered a season where the Lord will bring many of us into those anointed times of prayer, so we need to be ready when that happens. We can no longer pray prayers that are cloaked with old religious traditions, mindsets, or habits. God is lifting his Ekklesia to pray and decree in ways that we have never experienced before.

Let me return to the passage that is quoted above under this chapter title. Those verses states something extremely powerful that we need to embrace in this hour. Let's read them again.

> *Your marvelous words are living miracles;*
> *no wonder I long to obey everything you say.*
> *Break open your Word within me until revelation-light shines out!*
> *Those with open hearts are given insight into your plans.*
> *I open my mouth and inhale the Word of God*
> *because I crave the revelation of your commands.*
> *(Psalm 119:129-131 The Passion Translation)*

On Sunday morning, March 5, 2023, as I was preparing for our morning worship service, this passage was highlighted to me by the Lord. I don't think it was coincidence at all that it was on the eve of Purim where we are very aware of the decrees or declarations that needed to be made by Esther and Mordecai to save the Jewish people from the horrific plan of Haman. This passage is also a part of the lengthy Psalm which is divided up to represent each letter of the Hebrew alphabet. This portion of Psalm 119 is dedicated to the Hebrew letter "Pei." According to the Hebrew calendar, the decade of 5780-5790 (Hebrew Calendar) or 2020-2030 (Gregorian Calendar) is the decade of Pei. Hebrew letters have pictures that depict the letter and Pei is represented by the picture of a mouth. It is therefore the decade of the mouth. It is the decade

---

[11] *Return of the Priests: Discovering God's True Intent for His People* by Thomas Schlueter

when we need to open our mouths and release what God needs to release to set forth his Kingdom into the earth.

So, listen carefully to these words. The Lord says, "My words are miracles," and I will break open My word "until revelation light shines out," and that if you will open your mouth, you "can inhale My very word," and you will then have "a revelation of My commands." The Lord revealed to me that if we inhale His word, the next action is to exhale His word. That which has gone into us by revelation from His throne room must now come out through the declarations and decrees of our mouths as we pray. We just can't pray with the old religious standards and ideas and models that we've used in the past. We can't just "name it and claim it." We must be actively pursuing, as kingly priests, a revelatory and intimate relationship with our King so that when we do pray, we will be releasing what He has said to us and not what is our opinion, our thoughts, our ideas, or our reasonings about how things should be taking place.

The Lord's words are living miracles. We must crave the revelation of His commands!

This next portion is a little bit "tongue in cheek." For many years now I've been living, moving, and having my being among intercessors. Pardon the misuse of that passage, but I have attended an innumerable number of intercessory meetings. I've attended small ones and large ones. I've attended ones that broke out spontaneously and ones that were programmed with every little detail that had to be followed to move through the program. I have noticed many different styles and patterns of intercession. These prayer habits speak to me of a variety of people praying in a variety of ways, and most of the time it was because of the way they had experienced or were taught prayer by others. This happens to all of us. I can remember when I was growing up that there were certain patterns of prayer that were taught to me or patterned for me by parents, Sunday School teachers, or other members of prayer groups.

It's amusing now, but I can remember when I was a child how my style of prayer was my eyes closed and my hands in the traditional folded position lifted in front of me. I had seen this in pictures or paintings of Jesus in the garden. It was further strengthened by the instructions of teachers to fold my hands and close my eyes. I remember looking at other adults that were praying in the church and I saw them simply holding their hands down on the pew or even gently folding them in front of their bodies. I often wondered, "when would I get to do it that way?" It really messed with me in later years when I realized that I could, in church, lift my hands above my head to praise the Lord in prayer. I also discovered that I could keep my eyes open. John Wimber used to say, "if you keep your eyes closed during prayer, you won't see the miracles you're asking the Lord to perform." I know it sounds simple and silly, yet that's what we often do. We mimic or copy the other people that have been praying in our lives. We try our best to learn prayer by their example. I learned how important it was for me to often ask the Lord, "teach me to pray."

I have also noticed a possible inability for some people to ask the Lord for a changing or maturing of their prayer life so that it lines up with His Kingdom principles. As I was praying one day, I asked the Lord about this, and He gave me a list of different styles of prayer that are being used by His church. **PLEASE NOTE: I don't share these in any way to judge anyone that uses these methods, but I do believe that the Lord wants us to examine our prayer lives so that as His kings and priests, we will indeed pray with precision.**

- **The Teaching Prayer** – This is the need for a person to release a teaching through their prayer. Teaching needs to be released into the body of Christ, but when it is done in the middle of prayers being offered, it has the potential of halting the move of the Spirit. I prefer to bring teaching or information at the beginning of as meeting, and then pray that truth.
- **The Lingering Prayer** or "I Was Born Under a Wandering Star" – this person is just not sure what needs to be prayed, but they will set out on a journey of praying – hoping to find the destination.
- **God Is Not a Comma** – I always want to ask this person: "Do you know who you're talking to?" The words Father, Lord and Jesus are continually used in the prayer almost like one would overuse use commas in a sentence.
- **Around The Mountain She Comes** – Years ago the Lord had instructed me to provide a conference call opportunity for the intercessors of Texas to pray every morning. We've been doing this every day for over ten years. The Lord said to me: "Give me fifteen minutes." I said: "Lord, intercessors will not like this. They will want to pray for a longer time." His answer was interesting. "I do not want them to go around the mountain over and over until they know what to pray. I want to teach them to listen to Me and decree My truth."
- **I've Got It All Covered** – Some pray with an attitude that "their prayer" will sum it up and no one can possibly add anything else. Ouch! Help us, Lord.
- **The "This Is What I Want" Prayer** – Everyone has a list! We all have certain things we've been praying for. I remember something that happened years ago regarding my prayer life. I was very frustrated because I saw that some of my prayers were not being answered even though I had been praying them passionately for a long time. Silly me. I remember asking the Lord about this. And He was very gracious in His corrective words towards me. He simply said to me: "You need to understand that number one on your prayer list is number four on mine."
- **I'll Get to The Main Point Soon** – This one is like the teaching prayer, but the person is not trying to pray. They are trying to make a point.
- **The Great Mimic** - I remember a time when I was praying a prayer, and as I was continuing through it, I suddenly realized that I was praying very similar to

a style used by another leader in prayer. God doesn't want us to mimic somebody else. He wants us to pray according to who we are and what He has planted in our spirit. In other words, if I hear someone praying who is very demonstrative and loud in their declarations, it doesn't mean that I must jump on the same bandwagon. I need to pray with the way that God has released me to pray.

- **I'm Praying "In My Heart"** – No, in a prayer meeting, not everyone has to pray out loud. Many people are fearful of praying out loud because they just don't think it's going to come out right. That's how we grow in prayer. People many times don't want to try something new because they're afraid they're going to fail the first time, or the second, or third time that they do it. But again, that is how we learn how to do it, whether it's riding a bike, driving a car, meeting legislators in the capital, or praying decrees.
- **I'm Glad I Don't Pray Like Them** – I do not think I need to comment on this one.
- **I don't have or use a prayer book** – Many of us grew up in strong religious or denominational structures. Most of our prayers, especially in my background of Lutheranism, were prayers that were read or decreed out of prayer or liturgical books that were provided to pastors or parishioners. I will never condemn or judge anyone if they are reading prayers out of a book. As a matter of fact, many of us are doing that these days as we read decrees or declarations that have been written by other apostles, prophets, and teachers in the church. A good example of this are the many decrees that I have reread and reread and reread again that Dutch Sheets or his brother Tim have offered up as declarations for this season. I also strongly exhort and encourage people to read the prayers that are already written throughout the Holy Scriptures. What better way to decree what God has already decreed than to read what He has already decreed. There is a moment though, when we need to ask the Lord, "What do you want me to decree based on what You have revealed into my heart?"

Do not worry. I'm getting us closer and closer to where I'll reveal the revelation regarding tribunals. But it has been very important for us to understand who we are. And by what authority we can decree what God has already decreed. A major shift took place in my understanding of this when we were praying in the state capital of Texas in Austin. We've been doing this for several years but on this occasion, as we were praying for a couple of our leaders that we felt just were not moving in the direction that God needed them to move. We were praying, as we often do, for God to bless them, open their eyes, and change their hearts.

Suddenly, the Lord lifted me up out of the room so that I could look back down on the others that were praying. I was a bit frightened by the experience but then He clearly spoke to me and said, "I don't want you praying that way. Tell them to stop praying that way. You're dealing here with a pharaoh spirit, and it needs to be dismantled and removed."

As I found myself once again with the other intercessors in the room, I told them what I had experienced, and we immediately shifted into making decrees that dismantled the spirit of Pharaoh over our state and our nation. Not long after that, in a very surprising move, one of those leaders resigned his office for no apparent reason. The other leader was no longer able to pass his influence to a person that had already determined as the one to follow him in his plans.

Dutch Sheets, at one of our TXAPN Council gatherings in January 2021, commissioned us, as intercessory leaders in Texas, with these words:

"And I'm going to give a higher and stronger anointing mantle to this state to help Me (the Lord) disassemble and tear down and rebuild what I want in this nation. So, the Lord says, you back into Austin, you go back into that place again. You go again. I know you go all the time, but this is an assignment. You go in there. The Lord says, you go in and this time know that I have mantled you and I have given you an authority that you have never carried in there before to dismantle and to uproot and to demand replacing of people and a placing in of those I have raised up in this state to rule. I have built an Ekklesia and I'm about to use my Ekklesia to release them in levels that they have not yet walked in."

Prophet Lana Vawser from Australia wrote: "What the Lord said next to me shocked me. He said, 'You are a people with a storm in your mouths!' and at first, I honestly had no clue what He was saying. A storm? Aren't storms from the enemy? Then I found this scripture: 'Behold, the storm of the Lord has gone forth in wrath, even a whirling tempest; it will swirl down on the head of the wicked" (Jeremiah 23:19). God is the creator of storms like He is the one who in Isaiah 54 creates a destroyer to destroy the enemy's plans! You can't beat that!"

He is releasing His words through us. A popular meme on social media is a conversation between the enemy and us. It reads: "I am going to come like a storm to destroy you and the response is 'I AM the storm."

Let me close this chapter by quoting from the book, <u>Prayers Which Overcome Institutional Evil</u> by Apostle Jim Hodges, which deals with the concept of imprecatory prayers, which are prayers that implore the Lord God to destroy evil and to release His kingdom authority against unrighteousness. Dr. Hodges has been setting the standard of this kind of Kingdom prayer for many decades.

Considering what is happening in the Body of Christ, in our nation, and the nations of the world, the true Body of Christ must come to a new level of intercessory prayer. I believe that next level is the release of prayers which confront and conquer evil that is embedded in religious systems and government structures. A sizable segment of the Body of Christ is aware and to some degree involved in spiritual warfare. Much has been written about this important truth in recent years. We are aware that evil powers (the ones listed in Ephesians 6) are oppressing and to some degree governing the peoples of the earth. Where the oppression is the greatest is when these evil principalities, rulers, spirits of wickedness, and forces of darkness become embedded and expressed through religious systems and government structures. This study is about dislodging and defeating these evil entities.[12]

---

[12] Introduction, Prayers Which Overcome Institutional Evil, by Jim Hodges.

4

Tribunals – Part 1

When the king saw Esther the queen standing in the courtyard, she obtained favor in his sight; and the king extended to Esther the golden scepter which was in his hand. So, Esther approached and touched the top of the scepter. (Esther 5:2)

*Praise the LORD!
Praise the name of the LORD;
Praise Him, you servants of the LORD,
You who stand in the house of the LORD,
In the courtyards of the house of our God!
Praise the LORD, for the LORD is good;
Sing praises to His name, for it is lovely. (Psalm 135:1-3)*

*I kept looking
Until thrones were set up,
And the Ancient of Days took His seat;
His garment was white as snow,
And the hair of His head like pure wool.
His throne was ablaze with flames,
Its wheels were a burning fire.
A river of fire was flowing
And coming out from before Him;
Thousands upon thousands were serving Him,
And myriads upon myriads were standing before Him;
The court convened,
And the books were opened. (Daniel 7:9-10)*

Or do you not know that the saints will judge the world? If the world is judged by you, are you not competent to form the smallest law courts? Do you not know that we will judge angels? How much more matters of this life? (1 Corinthians 6:2-3)

I could be opening this chapter with two passages that basically have defined my life. If you have read any of my previous books, you will know that my last name, Schlueter, is an occupational name in German. Schlueters were "The Keeper of the Keys of the Prison." So, I could have easily gone to Isaiah 22:22 or Matthew 16:18-19 to release what needs to be taught regarding tribunals. Let's read them again.

Then I will put the key of the house of David on his shoulder;
When he opens, no one will shut,
When he shuts, no one will open (Isaiah 22:22).

And I also say to you that you are Peter, and upon this rock I will build My church (Ekklesia); and the gates of Hades will not overpower it. I will give you the keys of the kingdom of heaven; and whatever you bind on earth shall have been bound in heaven, and whatever you loose on earth shall have been loosed in heaven (Matthew 16:18-19, emphasis added).

I need to state up front that there is no intention here of the teaching on tribunals being the end of all things. Tribunals, as the Lord has taught them to us here in Texas, are an essential aspect of how He desires us as the intercessors in the Ekklesia of Texas to release His decrees and declarations into the state and, yes, into the nation, but the revelation of what tribunals release are present in many gatherings of the Ekklesia that are not called tribunals.

As we begin to define tribunals, let me quote again what I wrote in the Introduction.

One online dictionary rendered this definition. A tribunal is "a court of justice or any place where justice is administered." Words related to word tribunal include court of law, committee, judge, justice, bar, bench, council, forum, magistrate, and judiciary. Let's now put more meat on this.

Prayers That Shape Cities, States and Nations

Starting in 2022, I joined together with Greg Hood as one of his instructors in Kingdom University.[13] One of my subjects is to teach on the title of this section – "Prayers that

---

[13] You can go to www.greghood.org/kingdom-u.html to find out more

Shape Cities, States, and Nations." It is time to strategize and align prayer in each of our states. I am the team leader or coordinator of the Texas Apostolic Prayer Network of which oversees the 254 counties in Texas that have joined together as a well-oiled, fervent in prayer, Ekklesia.

I have been and continue to carry out a role as an apostolic leader in the state of Texas, but my role also includes being a coordinator at a national level with other states. Several years ago, the Lord gave me a word, "The strength of a nation is in the power of the individual states." And I would add that the strength of the state is in the citizens of the state.

Last year (2022), the Lord asked me the following question, "Have you considered the blade of grass?" He then began to reveal to me that in a grassroots movement, such as we see with TXAPN, that each blade of grass (you) is the most important part.

Interestingly, that is the very essence of who we are as a nation. We are not to see a federal government that oversees the states with unrelenting power and authority. The power of our nation is with the people and in the individual strength and giftings of each of the states. The same is true for any initiatives of prayer. I hope to lay out in the following pages a short but succinct message that you must hear what God is saying to you regarding your home, your church, your city, your county, or your state. Research where you live. Discover the giftings and the destiny of your assignment. Read books like <u>Releasing The Prophetic Destiny of the Nation: Discovering How Your Future Can Be Greater Than Your Past</u> by Chuck Pierce and Dutch Sheets.[14]

But most importantly, seek the face of the Lord and listen for His directions as you partner with God in His development of a grassroots movement across the nation. Our nation's destiny is at stake, and we can no longer depend on a few anointed leaders to carry out the task. God is raising up a grassroots army and you are enlisted, by His Spirit and calling, into that army.

Over the years, as a network of intercessors has been developing across the state of Texas, many have asked me, "How did you do it?" I sensed in their query that they were looking for a formula or a strategy that could be used in their own situation, whether that be in a city, a county, or a state. Some were merely wanting to hear a testimony. As you read the following pages, this is not a "how to" book even though we will share some protocols and principles. You will read about revelations that the Lord gave us regarding our assignments in the state. **The gathering and networking of**

---

[14] Published in 2005 by Destiny Image. Available through Amazon

intercessors happened as we obediently carried out what the Lord had assigned us to do. I (and we) said "yes."

It all began in January of 2007, before the network existed, when I heard the Lord speak to me. He commanded me to drive the circumference of the state of Texas and honestly, I wasn't sure of the purpose of that trip. But I said "yes." Little did I know that five months later I would be asked to lead a new network of intercessors for the state. And after I was commissioned in the state capital of Texas by Chuck Pierce in June of that year, my wife Kay and I started our trek. I had sent out an email to approximately three hundred people that I had as contacts for around the Dallas-Fort Worth area and across the state. As we started our journey, many of them asked if they could join us along the way by providing a meal or a place to stay, **and the network was birthed.** It wasn't my strategy. It was simply obeying the Lord's command. As we obediently carried out His wishes, He added to us, not only numbers, but more importantly strategies, assignments and initiatives that were meant to release His Kingdom in and through the State of Texas. And I cannot stress this strong enough – we have become a covenant group.

I encourage you, as you to read on, that you don't look for a formula. Look for Him – our Lord and King. Carry out what He commands you to do. No more delay. He is forming His Ekklesia into a mighty army. Saying "yes" to Him will open His strategies to you regarding all prayer initiatives, including tribunals.

There are no formulas, but there are protocols. As I have been on and have also led many prayer initiatives throughout the state and the nation, we depend solely on the Spirit of the Lord. He will direct us on what we need to do, when we need to do it, and where we need to do it. He needs to be the One with the formula. He needs to be the One with the strategy. But in carrying out those strategies, the Lord has made it clear that there are certain protocols that must be followed.

So, what are the protocols? Some of these are obvious protocols that are a part of carrying out tribunals or any other prayer assignments. But we must be careful that we are not dragging out old methods, ideas, and strategies from rigid religious backgrounds.

- **Stay in your assigned sphere.** We can fail and even be harmed if we go into assignments or tribunals presumptuously. We should not simply proceed indiscriminately, but where, when, and how He sends us. Each of us has a sphere that we have been assigned to by the Lord. We are to watch over and guard it. I mentioned this earlier when I was writing of intercession being "a position." We are in those positions or spheres so that God can release His strength and authority through us in the area that we live or work. I have personally been very sensitive to this as I have moved across county lines or state lines to do prayer assignments. I want to make sure that the Lord (or persons in those spheres) has granted me permission or authority. I live in Tarrant County, Texas, and right next to us is Dallas County. Many times, I did not feel like I had authority when I would cross over the county line going towards Dallas. That changed dramatically, when in a meeting, Prophet Cindy Jacobs stopped in the middle of her message and prophesied over me saying, "Tom, the Lord has given you authority in Dallas."

- **Line up with the Word.** As we declare and decree, we must line up with the testimony of all of Scripture. Dutch Sheets writes: "The Bible must be taken as a whole; no passage is meant to stand alone. Scripture is to be interpreted with Scripture. Also, we must avoid spiritual formulas. Those who try to apply spiritual truth as formulas will quickly discover that "the four easy steps to…" will not work. God does not want our walk with Him, or our understanding of His Word relegated to religious formulas, methods, or systems."[15]
- **Trust and obey.** Let the Lord establish His pathway for your tribunal. I've learned out of my own experience that I can't drag a personal focus into the meeting. People will say: "Well, we need to deal with this right now." We may need to deal with something, but let the Spirit direct your path towards that goal. One of the tribunals in the state has a group of intercessors that meet the day before, with the Lord, to determine what direction He wants to take when the tribunal meets the next day. Excellent, but whether you do it the day before or as the tribunal unfolds, let Him do it. Then obey Him. Oftentimes we will notice that people, when they come to the tribunal, have all sorts of ideas about which direction it may take based on their own personal whims or opinions. That can easily distract what the Spirit wants to do. The leader needs to be cautious of that. The Spirit may want to introduce another theme, but again, listen to the Spirit.
- **Worship.** I will probably disturb some religious bones as I talk about worship. Worship is obviously the most important aspect of everything that we do. As the Ekklesia, it is the heartbeat of what we do. It is the very nature of us to glorify our Father in heaven and to magnify the name of His Son and our Lord Jesus Christ. But once again, sometimes people will bring in "their" method or "their" style of worship which might fit well on a Sunday morning worship service where you're expected to lead worship with four or five songs and then proceed with the rest of the service. Tribunal worship is an integral part of the flow of the entire gathering. There may be some singing, but many times the worship is simply providing a prophetic and revelatory atmosphere to the meeting out of which the Spirit will speak to and through the members

---

[15] Dutch Sheets, GiveHim15, March 9, 2023

of the tribunal. Worship will help release the declarations and decrees. Worship leaders, during the tribunal, need to be aware of this so that they don't move into performance or trying to get people to act like they would on a Sunday morning. By the way, is that the way our Sunday morning worship time should even go?

- **No stages or platforms.** Speaking of performance. The tribunal is not a place for any one person or leader taking the stage or the platform and using it to control where things are going to go. When I am leading the tribunal that happens at our own house of worship, I feel that I am there more as a conductor of a symphony. I'm watching and praying and trying to ensure that every instrument has an opportunity to play their part. The greatest desire is to have everyone involved.

- **The grassroots.** So that leads us to the grassroots. This is about the people, the sons, and daughters of the Most High God, who make up the Ekklesia. The Lord is wanting each person to come into the meeting with their design and destiny. He wants them to hear and release what He is saying to them. Everyone has a part in bringing the nation or a state or a city into alignment with his Kingdom. This is not about one leader doing it all. One of the things that has frustrated me the most, being a part of national intercessory networks, is that in many cases a state is being led by one leader or a very small team of people doing all the work of that state. That's nonsense! A grass roots army needs to be raised up in each state and in each county and in each city. We can't do things like we used to. We must activate the people of God.

- **No teaching or testimonies.** The tribunal is not the place for people to start releasing teachings or testimonies. This has happened on a few occasions, and it is imperative that the person who is helping coordinate the tribunal kindly but firmly tell them to stop. The purpose of the tribunal is to hear the Spirit of the Lord speaking to His Ekklesia and then releasing those declarations and decrees that need to come forth from the people. Many times, as I lead, I simply ask the person to now decree what they've been speaking or teaching to shift them from a teaching mode into a declaratory mode. When I am teaching a group of people about the tribunals, and we begin to practice, I state this even more firmly. I call a timeout and instruct the people that that is not the direction we want a tribunal to go. Let me reiterate that the teaching or research that is necessary for the tribunal should have already happened before the tribunal starts. Then the group can declare from that information as the Spirit leads. Sometimes, as I'm leading, I use the first ten or fifteen minutes in bringing some of that teaching or instruction to the group.

- **Decrees and declarations.** Decrees and declarations. What are they? A whole book could be written on this one topic but let me see if I can bring a simple definition or understanding as I have been taught by the Lord. Declarations are simply a repeated truth that we are releasing into the atmosphere. Many times, this happens when we are reading scriptures. We may declare, "God,

You so loved the world that you came to save us and to redeem us from sin, death, and the power of the devil." Town criers would often yell the headlines that were printed on the newspapers they were selling. They were declaring what has already been stated. A decree, on the other hand, I believe, is something that the Lord Himself wants to establish and He needs a member of the Ekklesia to bring it forth so that it can be set into place. For instance, I remind you of what happened in the state capital when the Lord told us to no longer pray the way we were praying. He wanted us to move into decrees. We needed to decree the dismantling of the pharaoh spirit over our state. We decreed: "I command the eviction of those who are abiding by the Pharaoh spirit." We saw this happen recently in a tribunal meeting when we were given directions by the Lord, through His Spirit to evict a very unrighteous and evil mayor of a city. Our intentions are not to destroy that person or to curse that person. The Lord wanted that person evicted from their position. We decreed over a period of several minutes that that eviction would be taking place. Lo and behold, just a couple of weeks after that, the mayor lost a runoff and will no longer be in office. Regarding decrees, we turn to a familiar passage in Job 22:28. *"You will also decree a thing, and it will be established for you; and light will shine on your ways."* The Hebrew word for "thing" is "emer." I'm not sure why it was translated as "thing", but it translates as "utterance, speech, word, promise or command." The passage could read: "You will also decree an utterance, or a promise or command," and it will be established for you..." You will decree, says the Lord, what I have uttered, decreed, or promised.

- **How Long Should it Last?** Most of our scheduled a tribunals in Texas last anywhere from one and a half to two hours. It's extremely important again to simply listen to the Spirit. There's no reason that a tribunal could last just thirty minutes or an hour.
- **What Do You Do?** Hopefully it's not overstressing it again that we pay attention to the Spirit of God. The tribunal that we hold here at Prince of Peace House of Prayer in Arlington starts off with some worship and then proceeds with prayers, declarations, and decrees. Sometimes the decrees start off when the first note is played on the piano. Sometimes we worship for an extended period. We spend time in the presence of God. Most of the meeting is an intermingling of the two. Even though I am watching over the proceedings of the tribunal, we have an open microphone. So, anyone attending is not only welcome, but strongly encouraged to come and decree what they feel like the Lord has released to them.
- **Let the Spirit focus the prayers.** So, this one seems obvious. Let the Spirit focus the prayers. We are not to bring a "to do list" of the prayers that we think need to be prayed. We need to come into the meeting with our hearts

ready to be led by the Spirit and allow the Spirit to dictate through us what needs to be declared or decreed.

- **Relax and have fun.** I took a break from writing the book and I asked my wife Kay if there was a protocol that I was missing. She simply said: "They need to have fun." Then, she said: "Fun things can lead to revelation." I can't tell you how many times we have been on vacation or family excursions and the Lord drops down in the middle of it with a revelation that I need to release into the atmosphere. Kay and I do a lot of antiquing. It's always amazing the things that we find that the Lord then uses as a prophetic instrument. I remember that I was in Tupelo, Mississippi and we went into an antique store. I found two precious items – a World War One bugle and a set of handcuffs (I'm all about keys). Little did I know that in the meeting that followed our antiquing adventure, that the Lord said I need to release a new sound, and the bugle needs to be sounded as we go into war. He then went on to decree: "You need to lock up the spirits of religion and politics and no longer allow them access to the nation." Wow!
- **Eat.** As friends and co-laborers in the Kingdom read this, I can hear them laughing. Of course, you're going to mention eating. I'm known across the state as the one who posts pictures on Facebook of the meals that I have enjoyed at some restaurant. It might be the best hamburger, chicken fried steak, ribeye, or shrimp dinner that I've ever tasted, so, I must post a picture. But then I realized that the pictures that I was posting were not just pictures of food, but they were taken during a meal where I was celebrating with covenant friends from across the state. How many times did the Lord release His revelations and the purposes for the Kingdom as He ate with His disciples. Eating is one of the most important things that we can do to express and enjoy covenant with each other. It's around the table that we share ideas and prayers and strategies and hopes and dreams and everything else that God wants us to be a part of. Many times, around the table is when we are most relaxed. We just had a gathering of intercessors and leaders in a home in the southern part of Texas along the Gulf Coast. It was interesting, because as we started meeting that evening, the Lord wouldn't let us do any "religious things." He wanted us to fellowship with each other, eat with each other and enjoy His presence as He swept over us with His glory. So, I encourage everyone who has a tribunal meeting that at some point during the meeting or after the meeting, you sit down and eat together. Seal everything that has been done with a meal. Isn't that what communion is all about?
- **Report results.** Peter Wagner, a friend, and a mentor. who has now entered heaven's courts, always exhorted us that whenever we were carrying out an assignment or doing strategic meetings, that we look for the tangible results of what took place. Did anything change? Was there a shift that took place? Was there a tangible physical answer to the decrees?

I believe that you will see some of those tangible results as we read on in the next chapter. These are some of the testimonies from tribunals regarding what has happened in their midst.

5
Tribunals – Part 2

The L<small>ORD</small> says to my Lord:
"Sit at My right hand
Until I make Your enemies a footstool for Your feet."
The L<small>ORD</small> will stretch forth Your strong scepter from Zion, saying,
"Rule in the midst of Your enemies."
Your people will volunteer freely in the day of Your power;
In holy array, from the womb of the dawn,
Your youth are to You as the dew.
The L<small>ORD</small> has sworn and will not change His mind,
"You are a priest forever
According to the order of Melchizedek."
The Lord is at Your right hand;
He will shatter kings in the day of His wrath.
He will judge among the nations,
He will fill them with corpses,
He will shatter the chief men over a broad country.
He will drink from the brook by the wayside;
Therefore He will lift up His head.
(Psalm 110)

I have read and meditated on this passage many times over the last decades. It has become a passage that clearly defines what the Lord has called us to do through the Texas Apostolic Prayer Network. Today (March 7, 2023) as I was reading it again, the Lord said to me: "This is you. You are My judges and My rulers that I have established on earth. I have extended my scepter to each of you so that you can be the ones that determine the fate of the enemies that you rule during. You are indeed sons and daughters and kings and priests after the order of Melchizedek. I will continue to use My people, My Ekklesia, to carry out the force of this passage. So, rule in the midst of your enemies."

This is my Father's world,
And to my listening ears
All nature sings and round me rings
The music of the spheres.
This is my Father's world:
I rest me in the thought
Of rocks and trees, of skies and seas--
His hand the wonders wrought.

This is my Father's world:
The birds their carols raise,
The morning light, the lily white,
Declare their Maker's praise.
This is my Father's world:
He shines in all that's fair;
In the rustling grass, I hear Him pass,
He speaks to me everywhere.

This is my Father's world:
O let me ne'er forget
That though the wrong seems oft so strong,
God is the Ruler yet.
This is my Father's world:
Why should my heart be sad?
The Lord is King: let the heavens ring!
God reigns; let earth be glad![16]
(Emphasis added)

Why would I be quoting this old hymn at this point. I'm going to make a grand assumption which I believe is truth. I believe very strongly that from the moment of our conception God is already starting to impart to us the design of His Kingdom. So, even at an early age He began to release into us revelation of His plans and of His destiny, not only for our personal lives *according to Psalm 139, but for the grand design of His Ekklesia.*

---

[16] "This Is My Father's World" by Maltbie Davenport Babcock. Public Domain.

Tribunals   **Dr. Thomas Schlueter**

> *For You formed my inward parts;*
> *You covered me in my mother's womb.*
> *I will praise You, for I am fearfully and wonderfully made;*
> *Marvelous are Your works,*
> *And that my soul knows very well.*
> *My frame was not hidden from You,*
> *When I was made in secret,*
> *And skillfully wrought in the lowest parts of the earth.*
> *Your eyes saw my substance, being yet unformed.*
> *And in Your book they all were written,*
> *The days fashioned for me,*
> *When as yet there were none of them. (Psalm 139:13-16)*

I was in second grade and my mom was my Sunday School teacher. One of the things that she stressed was that we would learn certain hymns that were important for our spiritual growth. We had to memorize two or three hymns that year. One of them was "Holy, Holy, Holy." Another one was "Beautiful Savior" or "Fairest Lord Jesus." The last of the three was "This is My Father's World."

I have these three hymns on a worship song list on my iPhone that I will play when I'm taking long trips. Most of the songs on my list are choruses and worship songs from almost six decades that have set the stage for the release of God's glory on the earth. Tucked away in that list was "This is My Father's World." I was on my way to Austin and the song began to play. I began to worship along with it and as I did the Lord informed me that He is indeed "the ruler yet" and that "He reigns" and He will be "making the Earth glad" through the work that we are carrying out as His body on earth. He planted that song in my spirit a long time ago and today He made it come alive. I'm not usually accustomed to crying (sorry for lying) but at that moment tears welled up in my eyes.

I remembered a similar experience when I was on an assignment up in Northeast Iowa. I was standing on land that I had once run across when I was in second or third grade. Now, at the age of fifty-five, we were there in the same place to deal with strong demonic structures that were attached with that land. As I now stood on the land, I asked the Lord why He had brought me to this place. And He surprised me with His answer. He said, "I needed you to repeat what you had done when you were here in second grade when I had already determined, in my design for you, that you would be a strong apostolic influence in the nation."

That word was confirmed when I received an unexpected phone call, at that very moment, from a good friend and Native American apostle, Jay Swallow. He is now with the Lord, but he asked me on the phone, "What are you doing, Tom? I sense that there is an authority moving through you."

Tribunals – The "How To"

There's a principle here that needs to be understood before we answer this question. Our leadership council was having one of its annual gatherings in Fredericksburg, Texas. It was early in our history of TXAPN and there were about sixty of us that were gathered around the tables. As we began to worship and minister to the Lord, the Lord opened my eyes, and, as I looked at the council members, they were all sitting around the room on thrones. He revealed to me in that moment that we were to be, as his sons and daughters, His appointed judges on the Earth.

A similar thing happened with a group that we call "Elders at the Gate." In 2001, and it was on the day of the 9/11 attack on our nation, I was at a citywide pastors meeting. It was our practice to meet once a month for fellowship, prayer, and a meal. That day was particularly hard on us as we watched with horror what was going on in New York City and at the Pentagon, but after prayer, we pressed on with the strategy that we had determined needed to take place among the pastors of the city.

We were meeting once a month as an entire group, but we decided that we needed to encourage each other to meet in groups of five or six on a weekly basis. It would be called "Pastors in Covenant." The group of pastors that I started meeting with have never stopped meeting even though the members of the group has changed through the normal transitions of life. We continued to pray, encourage each other, and share a meal. One day, about seven years ago, the Lord interrupted our meeting and decreed to us that we were not there just for fellowship, but that He had determined that we would be "elders at the gate." At that moment, I had the same sensation that I had had when I saw our council members sitting on thrones. I realized the Lord's intentions for His church was more than just having good fellowship times, worship, prayer, and church activities. We were meant to be His judges, determined to declare, and decree what needed to be brought into alignment with His Kingdom here in Arlington, Texas as well as our county and our state.

I wrote earlier about what the Lord had commanded us to do when we were gathered as intercessors in the state capital. He exhorted us to move away from a certain type of prayer and to move into declaratory prayers. He was releasing the same principle imbedded in the idea of tribunals even though we had not yet used that term. I'm writing this because it's not **absolutely necessary** that we use the word "tribunal," but that it's extremely important that we understand that they are a part of God's design for his Ekklesia. So, as we talk about the "how to" regarding tribunals, we need to start with understanding that we are coming together to be seated as judges.

We know the promise that wherever "two or three are gathered together, God is in the midst of us."[17] Regarding tribunals it goes further. The Lord seems to be saying that wherever two or three pastors, cities, counties, or states come together, "I will give you rulership over that region." Tribunals may have an attendance of only a few people, but I believe that it is God's desire that they represent several cities or even counties. There is a synergy that needs to be present to release the strength of the decrees that will be made.

I remember years ago, as the Lord was beginning to reveal His purposes for the city of Arlington that He told me that "if He had fifty people from one church praying for the city that He would bless that city," but then He went on and said, "if I could have ten people from ten churches praying, I will transform the city." The same principle applies to the tribunals.

How often should we meet? Meet at the Lord's bidding. Most of our tribunals in Texas meet a minimum of once a month. One of our tribunals in meets weekly. Tribunals that take on a larger area such as several states might meet once a quarter. As the tribunals develop, we might see them meet for emergency gatherings. The Lord may also determine where you are to meet. Our Birthplace Region of TXAPN which includes Houston makes sure that they are meeting in other locations within their region. They do this to get persons from nearby counties to participate.

The Testimonies

East Gate Region

I believe we need to start with the East Gate Region of TXAPN. Many years ago, the Lord had declared that this was the primary gate for our state. It was in this region, which is our Northeast area of Texas, where all the pioneers, settlers, Native Americans, Spanish, and French all journeyed to and from Texas. The Birthplace Region has a similar anointing because of its location on the Gulf Coast.

But the East Gate is also a very significant spiritual gate as we have noticed that many times the blessings and or curses that have affected our state have also come through this same natural area in Texas. It should not be surprising that when the Lord finally told us "This is it" regarding the tribunals that it was after Kay and I had visited the gathering in Tyler, Texas – the East Gate Region.

---

[17] Matthew 18:20

Diane Kirkwood, who is one of the coordinators of the region sent me this report.

> God has been moving in East Texas after so long seeing nothing happening here. In 2020 we had someone from the Smith County Republican Party come up to speak at our meeting and asked for prayer for the party in Tyler. She said the leader of the Smith County party was out of town a lot and left a lot to do for his secretary, who is a Muslim. This was bothering a lot of people who worked with him in the party. Also, there was an election coming up and her group was wanting to elect someone else for his position. We prayed at that meeting for someone else to be elected.
>
> The next month we had two more people from the Smith County Republican Party come and talk to us about a Democrat from Longview who was coming to the Tyler meetings. That Democrat was said to have George Soros connections. The Tyler Party was very uncomfortable with what was going on.
>
> Our TXAPN group prayed and did spiritual warfare over the situation. (Author Note: This was the meeting we attended). We felt good after the warfare as did the three Smith County Republicans members. The next month the election was held and the person our group had prayed for won the leadership position and was in position as the Smith County Republican Party leader. The Muslim and democrat were both gone. I check in every so often and all is well in Smith County!

On a personal note, my wife Kay and I were so impressed with the meeting that we had attended that first time there in Tyler, that we decided to go back the next month. It was almost unbelievable when we were told that the declaratory prayers that had been made the month before had all been answered during that subsequent month.

I will go on to say that we attended two more months in a row. During the next month, there was a report regarding human trafficking in Smith County and the following month, success was again reported. After the declaratory prayers of the tribunal regarding the cells that were promoting human trafficking, it was reported that they too had been discovered and arrested. Diane, as well as her husband Kerry, and Gary and RaJean Vawter continue to report success after success following their tribunal meetings and other region-wide assignments.

Trinity Region Tribunal

Not long after we had experienced the East Gate Tribunal, we launched the tribunal in the Trinity Region which includes the counties that surround the cities of Dallas, Fort Worth, Denton, and Arlington. We have experienced the same powerful expression of

Tribunals   **Dr. Thomas Schlueter**

God's presence and the manifestation of His Kingdom through answered prayers regarding the region that we live in, as well as the state and the nation. The other reports in this chapter will speak of many of those victories but I desired this report to focus on a very important aspect of the tribunal – worship. My good friend, and apostolic leader, Jon Bunn, leads a ministry in Fort Worth. He also leads our time of worship during the Trinity Tribunal. I asked him to give his perspective on how worship contributes to the tribunal strategy.

He wrote on the power of worship in tribunal ministry and how it unlocks God's presence and victory.

> Tribunals have been a part of Christian tradition for centuries and have been used to settle various disputes within the church community. These courts are responsible for handling issues related to church law, such as disciplinary issues or conflicts between church members. By addressing these issues and upholding church standards and teachings, tribunals serve to protect the integrity of the church community.
>
> There has been a growing movement towards apostolic or kingdom ministry in recent years. This ministry places a strong emphasis on prayer, worship, and prophetic decrees as a means of releasing God's authority and power. The focus is on creating an environment where believers can experience the presence of God and receive revelation and direction for their lives. Worship plays a crucial role in this ministry as it is seen to foster spiritual openness and receptivity. As the Psalmist says, "Let the praises of God be in their mouths, and a two-edged sword in their hands" (Psalm 149:6 NLT). An interpretation of the Hebrew word "Pitshu" in Psalm 149:6 suggests it means "two-mouthed." This Hebrew interpretation is based on the idea that "mouth" ("pey") is similar in sound to "Pitshu," and in the Septuagint, the word literally means "two-mouthed." The context of the verse suggests a reference to speaking or proclaiming. Coincidentally, we are in the decade of "Pey" according to the Hebrew calendar, and tribunals with powerful decrees are on the front burner of the King's agenda. From this perspective, the phrase "two-mouthed" would mean that the praises of God are in the mouths of his people and that they have the power to proclaim His goodness and faithfulness to both believers and non-believers, as well as to powers and principalities. This interpretation emphasizes the importance of using our words to speak His truth and declare God's victory in the face of spiritual opposition.
>
> Through worship, believers can connect with God's presence, experience emotional, physical, and spiritual healing, and partner with His sovereign will

over the nations. Many people have reported experiencing breakthroughs in their lives during times of worship in these meetings. Worship is a powerful weapon in spiritual warfare, as it allows us to connect with the presence and power of God. Primarily, worship functions as a key to unlocking things in the atmosphere. In our meetings, it is often used to "tune the room" into Holy Spirit's frequency. It gets people into a place where they can hear from Him more clearly and be inspired by Him to read scripture, pray, decree, prophecy, or receive instructions from Him. It is an integral part and powerful tool in spiritual warfare. We see it as a way for members to connect with the presence and power of God and declare His goodness and faithfulness. As Psalm 149:6 suggests, the praises of God are in the mouths of His people, and they have the power to proclaim His truth and declare His victory against spiritual opposition.

Psalm 22:3 declares that God is enthroned on the praises of His people. This emphasizes that worship is not just a passive activity but an active one that can invite God's presence and power into our midst. As believers, we are invited to worship God and participate with Him in His reign and rule over all things. We are called to be co-heirs with Christ, sharing in His authority and power as members of His kingdom (Romans 8:17). When we lift our voices in praise, we declare God's goodness and faithfulness and acknowledge His sovereignty over all things. Ephesians 2:6 says believers are raised with Christ and seated with Him in the heavenly realms. When we lift our voices in worship, we acknowledge God's sovereignty and goodness and affirm our identity as co-heirs with Christ.

Revelation 4:1-11 portrays a picture of worship that shapes central aspects of our relationship with God and frameworks in our tribunals. John sees a vision of a great multitude of believers from every nation and tribe standing before the throne of God and declaring His praises. This vision emphasizes that worship is not just a passive activity but an active one that can unite believers from every corner of the world and usher in God's kingdom on earth.

In 2 Chronicles, King Jehoshaphat and his army were greatly outnumbered by their enemies. However, they turned to God in worship and prayer, and as they began to sing and praise, the Lord caused their enemies to turn against each other, and the battle was won without a single Israelite having to lift a sword. This powerful testimony and strategy often exemplify how worship can bring about victory in battle during our tribunals.

Vivian Hibbert, a prophetic voice, and worship leader, stresses the importance of worship in spiritual warfare, believing it to be a powerful weapon that can lead us to victory amid battles. In gatherings, the role of worship is critical in guiding the room in the direction the Holy Spirit wants to go. The sensitivity of the worship team to the leading of the Spirit is vital, and everyone has a role in facilitating the Father's will. It is important to pick up on key decrees, scriptures, prophecies, or instructions from the leadership to partner with the Holy Spirit in the journey. This often requires the team to shift the setlist, take risks in singing something unrehearsed, or sing "spiritual songs" according to the leading of the Holy Spirit. The role of worship in our gatherings provides the "sound" for warfare. Being in step with what the Holy Spirit wants at that moment is crucial to the success of the gathering. Ultimately, worship guides the room and is a means of participating in God's reign and rule over all things and is a vital aspect of our relationship with Him.

Overall, tribunals and apostolic ministry can be powerful tools for building up the church and releasing God's kingdom on earth. By providing a platform for justice, guidance, and spiritual transformation, these practices help individuals and communities thrive and grow in their faith. The use of worship as a tool for spiritual warfare and for participating in God's reign and rule over all things is a central aspect of tribunal ministry and highlights the importance of worship in our gatherings and our lives.

Plateau Region Tribunal

Jimmy and Martha Dusek, residents of San Angelo, Texas, and two of the coordinators of this region write:

> Our Plateau Region has been holding tribunals for many years. From these tribunals we have received many God assignments to go to many rivers, lakes, high places, Masonic Lodges, courthouses, schools, universities and military bases, and our southern border. In obedience to God's assignments we have decreed, staked the ground, released worship, built altars, and supported many political candidates and aided one of our region's military bases.
>
> A sect of the Fundamentalist Church of Latter Day Saints, led by Warren Jeffs, purchased land, and moved his sect-cult into our region. This cult was in our region and was extremely secretive allowing no outsiders to know what occurred within the sect's property. God instructed us to go, build an altar, and decree into this property and cult. Within six months the compound was raided because of a report of sexual abuse of minors. The Texas Rangers and other law enforcement agencies carried out this raid. The children were removed, the compound was searched, and eventually a trial was held resulting in the imprisonment of Warren Jeffs. He remains in prison today. This

incident made world-wide news. The property was seized by the state of Texas resulting in the remaining cult members leaving the sect or the state altogether.

Our tribunal was contacted by the Chaplain of Goodfellow Air Force Base, Lt. Col. Borger, to come and aid him through prayer. The initial incident was an active shooter on the base. God revealed His strategy for prayer and intervention in this situation which we carried out in the location on base where the event occurred. Lt. Col. Borger contacted the Major in the affected unit. The Major was amazed how accurately we were able to know what occurred during the incident. (Praise God for His insight) He asked to meet us, and, in the meeting, he related how his life and Christian walk had been impacted by our prayers. Lt. Col. Borger had us return regularly to pray with him and over the base. We assisted in many military functions at his request from, funerals, changing of the guard ceremonies, to the change of command for the base. We had access into many areas and personnel on base not usually open to civilians.

Recently, our Tribunal was instrumental in joining with pastors, groups, and citizens in lobbying our city council to have San Angelo designated a sanctuary city for the unborn. Through much prayer, God-inspired decrees, and hard work the proposition against abortion was included on the ballot for the November elections. The proposition passed by an overwhelming majority. This success was due to many Christians working together. We were just a part of this effort.

Our Tribunal has also gone to our southern border on God's assignments. Many times, we have stood on the banks of the Rio Grande and released the decrees God had directed us to release. While the illegal invasion remains an ongoing problem, we believe that God is at work and His angelic army is actively assisting in Border Patrol duties and exposing the work of the human traffickers. We have visited facilities housing these illegal people and spoken with the persons responsible for these facilities.

The Plateau Region Tribunal has worked with other TXAPN regions to release God's decrees and strategies into the Nueces Strip which includes most of the southern border of Texas. We have worked closely with a pastor and intercessor of Uvalde during the recent tragedy in the Uvalde Elementary School where nineteen students and two teachers were killed. A prayer event is being scheduled to include judges, sheriff, marshals, and city officials who are still dealing with the aftereffects of this tragedy.

Tribunals　　　　　　　　　　　　　　　　　　Dr. Thomas Schlueter

Out of the same Plateau Region, there is a friend and member of TXAPN, Patricia Graham, who lives in Goldthwaite, Texas. A tribunal sprung up spontaneously in her community following her obedience to the Lord. Here is her story:

> I was living blissfully in Wimberley, Hays County, Texas. My daughter and son-in-law lived in Austin. They then bought a ranch, a weekend get-away, in Goldthwaite, Mills County. So, we would all convene at the ranch about once a month, enjoying the beauty of the hill country and plateau region. Then my son-in-law bought a building on the main street of Goldthwaite with the idea of establishing an upscale restaurant. They have since moved here and he has opened the Fisher Street Bar and Grill. On New Year's Eve of 2018, out of the clear blue, the Lord spoke to me, "What are you doing?"
>
> Out of nowhere, I had one of "those" moments when status quo doesn't seem right anymore. I thought that I should sell a property I didn't want in order to buy a home I did want in Goldthwaite. Surely, at that moment, I didn't really think I would live in Goldthwaite full time, but I knew I needed to establish a presence here. Pastor Cody Haynes (I was going to church in Johnson City then) and I talked about this. He said that this is hard ground and he prayed that if I was to move here, then God would open the doors. Well, things went so smoothly and fast that I got scared! It was like a runway. But, by the end of June of 2019, I was a homeowner here. When I was first in Goldthwaite and didn't know anyone, I went to the National Day of Prayer on the Courthouse lawn. I sat next to TXAPN members, Lynne and Jack Garner – very likely the only two Spirit-filled people there. Then, in July 2020, my friend and I were talking about the state of affairs in this nation. He asked, "So, what are you going to do about it?"
>
> Off the top of my head, I thought of these things: 1) join TXAPN, 2) write articles for the local newspaper, 3) prayer walk the community, and 4) pay attention to local politics since this is where it all starts. In the fall of 2019, I had a dream that we were inter-breeding deer: the deer from Central Texas (Spirit-filled) with the deer of the Plateau Region (faith-filled.) Pastor Cody said that the deer represent the church. The church I have chosen to attend is High Mesa Cowboy Church in Brownwood. The pastor is Todd King. I had told him that I belonged to TXAPN. One day he said he had met someone from TXAPN and asked if it was OK to share my phone number. As it turned out, the man he had been fishing with was Jimmy Dusek! In August, a small group met in my home: the Duseks, Pastor Cody, and a few like-minded friends (not many Spirit-filled people here) met at my house. We prayed for the territory. I

would say the territory we prayed for is the TXAPN Plateau Region. A tribunal was born.

In October, the Lord spoke to a man in my church, Rusty Howell. Rusty was impressed that he had defiled the land by electing judges that did not represent the Kingdom of God. Rusty started with immense energy, passion, and effort to establish Constitutional Counties. He is such a positive person that I do not know the outcome of all his efforts, but I do know that he was able to cause the Brown County Commissioners to pass a resolution declaring that Brown County is a Constitutional County. Rusty also came to Mills County and, as a result of his visit, concerned citizens formed the Mills County Constitutional Citizens. We were not able to get our commissioners to pass a similar resolution, but we did have a voice in the elections. So far, we have two out of five commissioners who will support the resolution. In the meantime, we remain connected by email (over 200 of us) and we meet twice a month for classes on Patriotism being taught by Jana Primrose (based largely on David Barton curriculum.) She is also a member of High Mesa.

In June of 2022, the LGBTQ folks were planning to have a weekend event in Brownwood. Todd King, our Pastor, was very much a part of the efforts to derail this. The church mobilized by praying. As it turned out, the sponsor for the event backed out. The LGBTQ people were looking for another venue and were going to use the Convention Center in Early. Except, upon learning this, High Mesa booked the center for that weekend first. Rusty held meetings to gather all like-minded pastors together to form a Gate-Keepers group. That group continues to be intact and act on behalf of Brown County. The LGBTQ event had to move to another community.

It is my firm belief that Rusty Howell and the subsequent events were the result of our tiny prayer group that met in my living room. Pastor Cody, Martha and Jimmy, and a small group continue to meet in my home about four times a year. We continue to pray over this territory. Out of that, a small group of five has formed in Goldthwaite which now meets every week to pray for the community, territory, state, and nation. As for me, my little folksy articles in the local paper, the Eagle, are published pretty much every week, which amazes me! This paper will not publish anything political, so I try to write stories from history that teach a lesson about who we are as a people. Out of that, other opportunities emerged. The first is that I have written more political articles for The Buffalo Gap News. Additionally, I was asked by Sheriff Mack, founder of the Constitutional Sheriffs and Peace Officers Association (CSPOA) to submit some research on election integrity to be used in a video he presented at a convocation in Las Vegas last July. That information is now going to be included in a book being written. One of Sheriff Mack's books is

> Are You a David? The gist of the book is that God can use the most unlikely person, if they are willing to be used, to do big things. I guess I am a David. I say that because I was interviewed on one of Sheriff Mack's programs and the moderator said that I was a David.
>
> The point I wanted to make that day was that God can use the most unlikely, least public figure to impact our world. Here I am – a nobody from a dot on the map - and He has brought all these things to pass in this county and this territory. The lesson is that He can do this through me, He can use anyone! So, this is my story. If there is anything you can use, please feel free to do so. Thank you. Blessings, Patricia Graham

Indeed, Patricia, God is using His people – His grassroots people – to change the atmosphere of the cities, counties, state, and nation.

Central Panhandle Region Tribunal

Penny Simmons, our coordinator from Lubbock shares how the Central Panhandle Tribunal affected the victory of our "Sanctuary City for the Unborn" campaign. This movement started when a small town, Waskom, in northeast Texas (our East Gate Region), repelled an attempt to have a Louisiana abortion clinic come into their city. Their city council said "no" with a unanimous vote. Over thirty cities have now followed suit, but Lubbock is still one of the most powerful, wonderful, and exciting stories of the influence of an engaged Ekklesia.

> The Central Panhandle TXAPN Tribunal played an integral part in making Lubbock a Sanctuary City for the Unborn and moving the Lubbock area into becoming a Kingdom Center. But, to understand the development of the Tribunal, perhaps a brief history of our journey would be in order. In 2003 a group of intercessors came together to raise up a house of prayer in the city with the intent to make Lubbock a Sanctuary City/Glory Outpost. Many prophetic voices were prophesying that God's intent in the coming days was to create pockets of refuge and glory centers in cities. Mike Bickle, Bob Jones, Chuck Pierce, and others were urging the Church to pray fervently for an awakening and to address the cultural issues of our nation. Small groups of intercessors from different churches and ministries joined us to pray for revival, reformation, and for the hard issues that the main line Church was unwilling to acknowledge. We took our lead from the International House of Prayer in Kansas City to concentrate on apostolic intercession born out of worship, intimacy, and devotion to Jesus. The result was that we began to take on the controversial issues such as abortion, sex trafficking, sexual

confusion, and the slide towards paganism and liberal government and theology in our city and nation. The intercessory strength of our city began to grow. The intercessors and support for the HOP was a cross section of full time prayer warriors, business leaders, and amazing worship leaders most of which were the remnants of an attempt in the city to bring city-wide revival through the early Colorado Springs prayer movement. That movement had failed in the city as churches split and support faltered.

The remnant of intercessors, however, was vibrant and strong with leadership from some local Charismatic churches, Chuck Pierce, Mike Bickle, Lou Engle, and others keeping us alive with sound teaching and encouragement. In 2012 Chuck Pierce visited Lubbock and prophesied that Lubbock would one of 16 Glory Outposts in Texas. He said of the sixteen that four were the brightest and that Lubbock was among the four.

This confirmed to us that God was indeed honoring our prayers that Lubbock and the surrounding region would be a resting place for the Lord, a regional Tabernacle of David...a Glory Outpost. The intercessory force grew, though somewhat loosely with the House of Prayer (HOP) being a gathering place for prayer and teaching. When there was a threat to our city or a prayer gathering was called no matter where it was in the city the somewhat hidden intercessory groups that we often referred to as "likely suspects" always showed up to pray. Our relationship with TXAPN also grew as both TXAPN Regional Coordinators became partners with us and in 2016 we officially joined the network as our HOP Director became a council member.

Our partnership with TXAPN caused us to grow exponentially and expanded our focus. TXAPN provided a framework to draw diverse prayer groups together for prayer assignments for the state. It was a unifying vehicle for more focused intercession. Tom Schlueter led us so well in gathering our intercessory force to address issues, bringing unity of purpose and new covenant relationships. In 2020 Dutch Sheets and Tom orchestrated a move from TXAPN being a network of prayer to becoming a Tribunal with each region forming their own Tribunal group. We followed suit.

The stage was set, and in 2020 our strength was tested as Planned Parenthood attempted to return to the Lubbock area. Our tribunal turned our cannons towards the threat and began to meet as a military type of unit to stop the invasion. We quickly joined with a prayer group who we now refer to as the five Grandmothers, Texas State Senator, Charles Perry, Former Texas Solicitor General, Jonathan Mitchell, and East Texas Right To Life Director, Mark Lee Dickson. They had come with a strategy to fight Planned Parenthood Lubbock (PPL) - the Sanctuary City Ordinance. Our Tribunal boarded a plane and went to the capital to pray with Senator Perry. He said something I will never forget, "If there is a threat to your city and God gives you a remedy, we are compelled to use it. God will hold us accountable." He was speaking of the Sanctuary City Ordinance, but the same can be said of the Tribunals. God has given us a remedy for threats to the Kingdom.

The Central Plains Tribunal was called together along with the Northern Panhandle and Permian Basin. Tom led us as we decreed and declared life into our city. The Central Panhandle Tribunal continued to pray and decree, but something else was happening. As the campaign for life progressed so did our numbers as God began to reveal the Ekklesia in the city. We were finding each other. Small prayer groups, ministries and government and business leaders joined us. I believe they were seeing the power of informed, spirit led intercession and our authority to declare and decree with results.

Our victory over PPL and the establishment of Lubbock as the largest Sanctuary City for the Unborn in the nation became a reality. But. we were nor finished. Despite our conservative reputation in the Panhandle Region, Texas Tech University (TTU) and the TTU Health Sciences Center are centers for systematic leftist indoctrination. And there is a growing encroachment of liberal ideology among the "elite" influencers in our city. The battle at our gates for the Sanctuary City revealed the stark reality that Lubbock leadership had gone woke.

Through our Tribunal, we had seen the merging of the government and business mountains into the Ekklesia. As Senator Perry had said God had given us a remedy and now another vehicle to tackle problems with not just prayer, but action. It's a reality that normally after a victory that most warriors go home. This was not the case in Lubbock. I believe that can be partially credited to the formation of the Tribunal.

We went to work on replacing our mayor, city council members up for election, and a state representative. We also influenced the outcome of our school board election to save our conservative members' seats challenged by a super liberal PAC. We triumphed with godly candidates for all positions.

We have been trained well by Tom, Chuck, Dutch and many others and remembered always that we are fighting from a place of victory. The battle has been hard fought, but we are winning.

The Sanctuary City campaign had brought together new partners for our Tribunal from the business and government spheres, and it also revealed and brought together prayer warriors from various city prayer groups, church partner prayer groups, and local expressions of ministry groups such as Justice Foundation, 10 Days of Prayer, Project Destiny, 4 West Texas, and Citizens for Education Reform all who are focused on local, state, and national issues. Our common denominator and unifying factor is that all follow Chuck, Dutch and embrace TXAPN. All understand our authority as the Ekklesia. This added to our Tribunal. We went from about 12 to 40, with these seasoned leaders representing over 120 intercessors.

We knew the battle to fulfill Chuck Pierce's word for the region to become a Glory Outpost would take winning every mountain of culture in our city, so our next and current target is our public schools and university. Just as God highlighted His choices for public office, He highlighted people on the Education Mountain to lead our efforts to expose unbiblical programs and reform our schools. The Citizens For Education Reform was birthed. CFER trains parents on what to be aware of in their child's studies and report abuses. It investigates curriculum and lobbies in Austin for change.

God is surely building His Ekklesia. For the Central Panhandle, we feel we are just scratching the surface of what God wants to do. All we have accomplished so far could not have happened without the understanding of our authority as believers and God's desire to build and equip His Ekklesia. I believe all that we have done was birthed out of prayer, action, and legislating through our Tribunal.

Birthplace Region Tribunal

The Birthplace Region includes the counties of Austin, Brazoria, Fort Bend, Galveston, Grimes, Harris, Montgomery, San Jacinto, Walker, Waller, and Washington. As the Tribunal formed in this region, it took on a multi-region format. Darla Ryden, one of the coordinators of this region, wrote the following:

> In October 2021, we meet in Dickinson, Texas (Galveston County) for a restructuring of the birthplace regional tribunal, as collectively we had tragically and unexpectantly lost our leader, Mary, and her husband, Ken Bostrom, to covid in August. Mary was a skillful teacher of the gospel, and her years of teaching and training brought her in contact with many different ministries making her a remarkable gatherer when the call went out to rally. So, this assembly was to try and pick up the pieces of a diverse group that was connected to Mary, but not necessarily to each other. Tom Schlueter had come

to assist us in this transition and to provide us with fresh vision for the tribunal. The gathering was exceptional.

On the ride home from the meeting Debra Marshall, from Huntsville, Texas (Walker County) shared the following revelation, *"I saw in a vision a rider on horseback as in Paul Revere and I heard the word "Circuit Rider". He was riding spreading the word and sounding the alarm throughout counties in the Texas Birthplace Region. The rider was carrying the word of the Lord and that word was a fire or flame igniting each county as he went. Those that would hear and respond to this alarm would awaken and rise to become "Circuit Riders" themselves taking this fire of revelation to new areas. I also sensed such a great move of unity and responsibility for this call."*

Well, this revelation set us on a course of discovery and encounter with the Lord. November 2021 and January of 2022 we met in Houston, Texas (Harris County). Then in February we were invited to bring the tribunal into Cleveland, Texas (Liberty County) which is not within our region, however Holy Spirit was directing our steps and we wanted to respond to his leading, so we followed.

March and April found us back in Houston then May carried us to Huntsville. Then in June we again were taken out of our region into Bryan, Texas (Brazos County) which helped to kickstart an incredible gathering of pastors and intercessors in that region. We truly were becoming Circuit Riders, carrying our declarations and decrees with us wherever the Spirit directed.

July, we circled back around to Cleveland, Texas and since then the region is exploding with new expressions of the Kingdom. A monthly gathering called, *Advance*, just started this month (March 2023) to seek revival, reformation, and transformation. We are believing for a great move of Holy Spirit, as there have been many prophetic words proclaiming that the rural areas of Texas would be first to ignite with His presence and fire, so we are pregnant with promise! We traveled back to Houston for the August tribunal and started to see a pattern of going out to win a battle and then returning to the base camp to strengthen the troops, gather new supplies and rest the horses for the next journey. It was just so fascinating to follow Holy Spirit instead of lead, though we were leading, if that makes any sense!

September was a complete surprise, we gathered three larger TXAPN regions together; Birthplace Region, the Valley Region, and the Coastal Bend Region, in Victoria, Texas (Victoria County). Again, we assembled because of a few prophetic words spoken over the regions declaring our need to come together.

By this point, we were recognizing that we, as the watchmen of the state of Texas, were shifting from having our individual territories, into a corporate body operating as "ONE," as "FAMILY." Totally dependent on each other, not competing but deferring one to another. Where the need was greatest, we all rallied to overthrow, overpower, and occupy!

By the time we closed out October and November in Houston, we were exhausted not only because of the Circuit Riding across the state, but also because Texas had been moving throughout the nation the entire year as well. The nod from Holy Spirit of a job well done, came when the Houston Astros won the World Series, on November 5, 2022, and a prophet that consistently interprets the meaning of the winning team had this to say, *"The win in Houston goes to the INTERCESSOR!"*

The Birthplace region is named this because we are the region that birthed the Republic of Texas, not the state, but a nation (republic) and that is exactly what we are doing as the watchmen of the greater Houston region, we are causing new life to come forth all over the state. We know our job, as a midwife, is to help deliver and then circle back around to assist the family with anything they might need to expand and grow their territory into the fullness that God intents it to be. We know who we are and whom we belong to, and we will ride on using our authority to see Texas birth the nation that is within her loins so that a nation (United States) can be saved!

Capital Region Tribunal

As I mentioned earlier, each Tribunal takes on its own nature as those participants listen carefully to the Spirit of God. Nicole Smith, one of the coordinators of our Capital Region, gives this testimony from Auston, Texas.

> We were given a prophetic word by Clay Nash, and he told us that The Lord was inviting us to circle Austin seven times for the first seven months in 2022 and if we did, we would see the liberal agenda come down like the walls of Jericho did. We value prophetic words and prophetic acts just like Ezekiel did, so we assembled teams in the North, East, South and West parts of Austin and we hit the ground running calling it the Jericho Assignment for Austin Kingdom Gateway!
>
> We first started with a Zoom call where we all shared our prophetic insights of our Region and got a good bigger picture of what God had already done in this city and what He wants to do here, then prayed and blessed our Region. We then went out seven times a month to pray, decree and declare what we heard God saying in the places that He told us to go. Binding, losing, pleading

the blood of Jesus, and taking authority over our land, families, businesses, governments, and churches. I quickly realized that these were "Mobile Tribunals", so we decided to end with a formal Tribunal on July 7, 2022.

Many other leaders, friends and our TXAPN Family drove from all over the state to be at this Tribunal. It was incredibly powerful, and we called it "the merging of the streams of ministry into the River of God" It was beautiful. It was powerful. It was a covenantal family joining together to see the Governmental Region of Texas saved. Just days after the end of the seventh month had ended, I got a news notification that a local store called "Lucy in Disguise", just one mile from our State Capitol Building, had announced its doors were closing after 38 years of being in business! This business was dedicated to serving the LGBTQ community, witchcraft, and new age ideologies. I knew this was not a coincidence for a few reasons. First, in the original language, Hebrew, there is no word for coincidence which means that God is always orchestrating our events, especially when we are obedient to His word and will. Secondly, the Lord moved me to Austin to pray for justice and righteousness in our land and this happened in my 38th year of life! Coincidence? I think not! We can trace all this back to our Tribunals! I knew I was born for such a time as this and so are you! Many signs, wonders and miracles have transpired since!

A major prayer point of our Tribunals has been the Business realm. As we saw an influence of people flooding into Austin and bringing their false gods with them, we decreed that God would bring righteous business people here who have the financial power to change our city and that others would encounter the true Lord Jesus Christ and renounce their other gods for The King of kings and Lord of lords! Elon Musk was a high person of interest for prayer as he was in the beginning stages of building the Tesla plant and had recently moved his Corporate Headquarters here to Austin. We knew he would be recruiting people from all over to come and work here so we interceded for the employees and for Elon to encounter the true Lord Jesus Christ and serve Him and Him alone. So, during the Jericho assignment we went on two occasions to the Tesla plant to decree and declare, to allow and disallow, open and close. It was my great joy and was so elated when I found out that a man we were praying with and helping, who was experiencing homelessness, got a job at the Tesla plant! Towards the end of the Jericho assignment for Austin Kingdom Gateway Tribunals, Elon purchased Twitter and that quickly became the source for truth on a social media platform as well as most other new sources! He uncovered many "Twitter Files" exposing corruption in the American Government who worked with news outlets to falsify information to the public, we found out that the company had censored truth from coming out including the origins of covid and lockdowns! Much more is still being uncovered by this billionaire from the business realm that God is using to change the course of evil that was unleashed on the Nations!

Also, the Lord just connected me with a business person who all the sudden decided it was time to move to Austin Texas from another state! This person has a heart to shift this city for the glory of God, to see the power of darkness dispelled and has the financial power to help! This person has 3 million followers and just "randomly" decided to trust me, an unknown maid servant who God poured His Holy Spirit into this flesh, to anoint the new home they purchased and build a relationship. Coincidences? I think not! We can trace all this back to our Tribunals!

We also pray for the Church realm in our Region. We live to see the dismantling of the spirit of religion and see the Body of Christ move in the power of Holy Spirit as one! We decree and declare that that the people of God in our Region will move in the power of the Gospel of the Kingdom of God not religion. Furthermore, there must be action steps with our prayers of faith. So, I signed up to start the Austin campus as a coordinator for Kingdom University with TXAPN the same month that we started the Jericho Austin Kingdom Gateway assignment. The Lord told me to start an oikos family, not another program. So, we did, and we have people who come from all over the Region, some driving two hours to get here! I told God I would do it even if it was just me and with that yes from me, He created a small but powerful family and army with us! The teaching we receive isn't being taught in any of the churches that I have previously been to and were just all so hungry for truth, hungry for freedom, hungry for the power of God to be made manifest in our midst! The knowledge we've gained is shifting religious paradigms and empowering our students to live victorious lives as we take authority over the enemy in our lives, families, cities, states, and nations! We realized that we had been allowing religion to hold us down and shut our mouths, so we all decided to get rebaptized, but this time we were getting baptized into the Kingdom of God! At this baptism we declared that we had come fully out of religious mindsets, structures, and limitations of American Western Christianity. We proclaimed that we serve but One God and His name is Jesus Christ of Nazareth who came in the flesh, and we decreed will we never bow to another again! We saw oppression leave, we exposed false prophets in the church and called them to repent, we saw healing from past traumas and great deliverances! As a family, we help each other when we are sick, we pray together, we laugh together, we cry together, we washed each other's feet and we've seen great victories in our midst. We now have two classes and are looking forward to seeing more miracles in the days to come! We are small but we are mighty!!!

One student reported, "My entire life has completely changed, and I am free! It's all due to you asking me to join the class!" Coincidence? I think not! We can trace all this back to our Tribunals!

Another prayer point for our Tribunals has been the concern regarding enormous amounts of drugs coming through our borders. On the fourth of July, we went to Kerr County, which is part of our Capital Region. While we were there, we uncovered a historic property filled with pagan items and false gods from around the world, so we demolished them and worshiped the Lord Jesus. We later heard of eight million dollars worth of narcotics seized in Kerr County and arrested eleven people!!! Coincidence? I think not! We can trace all this back to our Tribunals!

Lastly but certainly not least, we always pray for our government. Austin is the seat of Government for our state where all our laws are signed, so we decree that justice and righteous will come forth from our land! We pray for righteous and bold leaders who are filled with Holy Spirit to lead the charge and that even ungodly leaders would encounter Jesus through dreams, visions, and laborers on their path. This year, we learned of a State Representative from Montgomery County, the county I lived in prior to God moving me to Austin, decided that he will sponsor prayer and worship in the Capital every week during this 88th legislative session!

One of my Spiritual Fathers, Bob Long, has worked and ministered at the Capitol for twenty years and this is the first known time that anything like this has happened! We know that one the English words used for intercession is the Hebrew word "Paga", which means to encounter. We also know that we enter His gates with thanksgiving; and His Courts with praise according to Psalm 100! So, a Governmental leader has all the sudden just decided he was going to sponsor an encounter with the Living God, in the same building as laws are being decided on, each week to petition The Righteous Judge of Heaven as we enter His courts with praise on behalf of Texas so we will be a state whose laws honor our King Jesus! We also have bold leaders bringing forth legislation to protect our children from sexual predators, continuing to protect the lives of unborn babies in the womb, fund adoptions, keep foreign nations from purchasing our land and so much more!

Last November, we had an election for the Mayor of Austin. The body of Christ has been praying for a righteous Mayor for our city and though the candidate I and many others voted for did not win, the Lord gave me peace about the new Mayor. He said, "I will use this Mayor for My glory and I will tenderize the heart of this man." I was just informed that a local church requested a prayer session with him and not only did the new Mayor rapidly accept the invitation, but He also wanted it! There have been many failed attempts to pray with our former Mayor with no response at all or a "yes" that never happened.

Let us never forget and constantly rejoice in the fact that on June 24, 2022, Roe vs Wade was overturned, and we are now, finally, a post Roe Generation! This demonic legislation, that started in the courts of Texas, was responsible for murder of more than 63 million unborn American babies, couldn't make it to its 50th year... Selah! Coincidences? I think not! We can trace all this back to our Tribunals!

In closing, I think one of the greatest outcomes of our Tribunals for the Austin Capitol Region, was that we activated the Ekklesia to move in power as the legislative body of Christ to get us out of our pockets of individual ministry streams, and into the river of God, working together as a covenantal family, to see the ancient ruins of this City and Region rebuilt for the glory of our Lord according to Isaiah 61! What the Lord has done to connect us is so deep and we will never be the same and neither will our city or Region! The best is yet to come! Truly the Lord is in our midst and Austin shall be saved! Texas shall be saved! America shall be saved, and the Nations shall be saved in Jesus' name Amen!

On behalf of the entire Austin Region and Texas, I would like to honor and thank my Spiritual Parents and Apostle Tom and Kay Schlueter for your YES to the commissioning of Texas Apostolic Prayer Network, which has been one of the vehicles that the Lord used to shift an entire state for the Glory of our King Jesus! Thank you for empowering the Ekklesia in Texas! We love y'all!

Big Bend Region

Our dear friend Carmen Johnson and her husband Fred are faithful guardians of El Paso, Texas, and the long border with Mexico. She is one of coordinators of this TXAPN region but also coordinates the Border Prayer Network along with New Mexico, and the Eagles Force Prayer Call. She writes...

> The Region 7 Tribunal, which includes El Paso, Brewster, Hudspeth, Culberson, Presidio and Jeff Davis Counties, was a full house gathering at the beginning, but since the beginning of the school year of 2022, it has come to a one hour

prayer gatherings twice a month and conference calls every Wednesday for thirty minutes. Our team consists of Carmen Johnson – Council Member of TXAPN and coordinator of two other prayer calls, along with Gina Castro – Council Member of TXAPN, together with eight to twelve others that periodically attend.

We have seen Holy Spirit progress in firing our city manager, who was running the city of El Paso into bankruptcy. Then a Former State Representative is now suing the Electric Company for excess increase in utilities. Our city has been the highest in taxes and highest in Utility costs, beyond the state average, way too long. We know God hears our declarations and decrees, so in faith we continue as Holy Spirit gives us revelation and insights as to what to pray.

Being a border region, we have, on the downside, seen an overabundance of immigrants cross our border along with criminals, felons, scoundrels, and the like, cross into the United States. Our tents and centers are overcrowded with families being separated and not enough officials to care for them. The immigrants wait for relatives, throughout the states to "adopt" them. When they get adopted, then they fly to their destinations. This also includes a three-month pay for whatever they need.

God is Holy, omnipotent, and omni-present and He knows what is going on. "The Lord gave the word; great was the company of those that proclaimed it" (Psalm 68:11). He wants to hear His word pronounced over this land. We intercede for our region and although it is scarce in population, it is God's country.

God is making this land a righteous and just land. We have seen Angels all along the border shoulder to shoulder protecting us. But now it is time for action. May God give those and us in leadership insight as to what needs to be done to stop this influx of people.

We are currently praying for HIS Glory to manifest first in us and then in our leadership.

One of the most powerful demonstrations of God's answer to our decrees happening in the community of Sunland which lies directly on the border of Texas, Mexico, and New Mexico along the Rio Grande. I stood at that point with Carmen a few years ago. Other than an international obelisk marker determining the line between two nations, there was no wall or fence. The Rio Grande is narrow at that location and was a major portal for anyone to enter the states illegally. A border patrol officer had followed us to the location and asked what we were doing. We told him that we were there to pray, and he said, "Yes, please." We dropped a plumbline and decreed that a wall would be built. Earlier that year I had personally donated money to a "Build the Wall" campaign that was raising funds to create walls along the border. Little did I know that the wall they were building was on the very spot were Carmen and I stood. There is now a wall along that border.

Carmen and her teams have also witnessed the total removal of abortion from the city and are now working with New Mexico to make sure abortion does not flourish there.

Indiana, Illinois, Kentucky, and Missouri

In 2022 I received at least three prophetic words that the Lord was going to begin to release the strategies and revelations that He has given to Texas into the nation. Again, I want to stress that the Lord said to me that He would use Texas for this purpose if we embraced humility and covenant instead of pride and independence. Not long after those prophetic words were spoken, the door swung wide open. I was teaching for Greg Hood at one of his Kingdom University gatherings in Franklin, Tennessee, and Craig and Kimchi Blow, students in the class, heard me speak about tribunals. Here is their report.

> The day we heard Tom Schlueter speaking in our Kingdom University classroom about Texas Prayer Tribunals, we knew we were supposed to start one in our state. We had developed something similar in our hub, but Tom's explanation and insights made it all come together on an elevated level. Tom is a natural, organic teacher with the astounding ability to father the prayer movement. We connected with Tom and Kay, and within months, we launched the very first tribunal in Indiana together. Tom's passion for prayer, his experiences, and his ability to share lessons learned brought excitement and the confidence to move forward in what our Father is doing in this new season. Tom clearly articulates the vision as it aligns with scripture. He propels the body to run as the true Body of Christ and express itself with freedom and integrity. His teaching provides discipleship and guidance, training others to follow the leading of the Holy Spirit in Christ's authority. He is a true apostle with a shepherd's heart.
>
> We were excited and honored to work alongside Tom, and, not to mention, be the very first state outside the great state of Texas to launch tribunals! We laughed and celebrated because Indiana is known as the "First Strike State." In this season, there is a divine relationship happening with Indiana and Texas. After our first tribunal in October 2022, it was obvious that God was doing more than just linking our state with these powerful meetings, seeing there were four states represented that day—Indiana, Illinois, Missouri, and

Kentucky. We naturally birthed a Midwest Regional Prayer Tribunal. Since then, leaders from each state have continued working together, hosting a tribunal in each location.

As the leaders brought the regional Ekklesia together, we saw an explosion of Jesus on many levels. The unity and oneness experienced in the room was nothing short of love, authority and power being released on levels we could tangibly feel. We were greatly encouraged to see the Body of Christ functioning organically and naturally together! Each person present exercised humility and honor. We witnessed all the unique parts, gifts, and anointings expressed like a perfect crescendo! We all fit together in this corporate armor with each of us holding an important part of the strategy to impact the war in the atmosphere!

We have seen the impact of our meetings. While in Carbondale, Illinois, we received immediate evidence that the prayers were working, as we made decrees as kings and priests. During this meeting, we saw the demonic entities over Chicago coming down; so, we agreed together in our authority to declare those evil and false structures were torn down. Within 30 minutes into our intercession, Tom received a news update that the spy balloon that was detected over our nation for a week had been shot out of the sky. We all knew our prayers engaged the enemy's camp and brought victory! We made specific decrees that day as the Lord showed us, locking in on the enemy's strategy. In fact, within a few weeks of that same meeting, a leader in Chicago lost her political seat and would no longer rule in Illinois. Yet, another knockout blow to the enemy!

We are nothing but encouraged by these tribunals. Since starting these meetings, we can gather the night before with just the key leaders for an apostolic round table to gain understanding of important events in each state, while learning about the hearts of our fellow leaders. This gathering has brought us together in intimacy and support so that when we meet the next day for the official tribunal, we see the unity of the spirit connecting us as one.

For us, the prayer tribunals are more than just another prayer meeting. It is like entering a command-and-control center with powerful spiritual leaders where Jesus is the Head. We understand what spiritual warfare is and the authority Jesus delegated to us. His example was that He sees and hears what His Father was doing in heaven, then He speaks and acts. In these meetings we have access to the corporate, united power within the whole body. There is something to be said about that. Until you experience that level of anointing, it is hard to truly understand the access we have to God's war room treasury right now as His standing Ekklesia.

She is very much a warring bride, alive, prepared, and ready to do battle on the frontlines. Working as a part of the tribunals, and with Tom and Kay Schlueter, has been a true honor. These tribunals have done nothing but help inspire and encourage us to be the kings and priests we are called to be. We are breaking out of the mold of religion and experiencing the Body of Christ operating as God intended.

We honor all that Tom and Kay have brought to us, our state and region, along with the many members of the corporate body through these prayer tribunals. We are now exercising the power we hold in prayer as Kings and priests who can decree a thing and see it happen!

Other Tribunals

As the multi-region tribunal developed in the Birthplace Region, we have seen the development of something similar between the Valley, Mission, Plateau, Heart of Texas, and Capital Regions moving together. We also have tribunals meeting in Victoria, Corpus Christi, College Station, Waco, Killeen, and Granbury.

6

Don't Listen to the Forever Loser

Then he showed me Joshua the high priest standing before the angel of the LORD, and Satan standing at his right hand to accuse him. The LORD said to Satan, "The LORD rebuke you, Satan! Indeed, the LORD who has chosen Jerusalem rebuke you! Is this not a brand plucked from the fire?" Now Joshua was clothed with filthy garments and standing before the angel. He spoke and said to those who were standing before him, saying, "Remove the filthy garments from him." Again he said to him, "See, I have taken your iniquity away from you and will clothe you with festal robes." Then I said, "Let them put a clean turban on his head." So they put a clean turban on his head and clothed him with garments, while the angel of the LORD was standing by. And the angel of the LORD admonished Joshua, saying, "Thus says the LORD of hosts, 'If you will walk in My ways and if you will perform My service, then you will also govern My house and also have charge of My courts, and I will grant you free access among these who are standing here (Zechariah 3:1-7).

It's Tuesday, April 11, 2023, as I am writing this. This morning, the Lord visited me as I was reading my daily Bible readings. I was in Zechariah 3. After listening to the passage, it was time to prepare for our daily fifteen minute TXAPN prayer conference call. But before I started the call, I read the morning post by Dutch Sheets on GiveHim15. I encourage you to look up these recordings from April 11-13. My heart was stirred up even more. After arriving at my office, I proceeded in recording my weekly "Tom's Take" on Facebook. Here is my edited version of what I recorded.

Good morning, everybody. This is Dr. Tom Schlueter with this week's Tom's Take. As we begin this morning, I know that many of you that listen to me on a weekly basis already do this, but I'm going to strongly encourage you again to make sure that you follow my friend Dutch Sheets' daily (Monday through Friday) as he posts his GiveHim15. Today and the next couple of days are going to be extremely important ones to listen to, to read, and to meditate over. I'm not going to share what he shared, but it's going to fall in line with what I want to share this morning. We are in that place now where the Lord is moving us into a place of victory and triumph.

Now that doesn't make sense, does it? As we're looking at the world around us, it's like, "what is going on?" I've mentioned this many times and I do not want to dwell too much on it here, but there is such a tragedy and travesty of injustice that is taking place in our nation. We are off course. I want to say right up front that I'm not coming to you from a political point of view. I'm not coming to you as a Republican or a Democrat or an independent. I'm coming to you as a son of the Most High God, a friend of God, as one who, along with you, has been anointed for this season to bring forth a manifestation of God's Kingdom into this mess.

We are seeing all sorts of travesties. Things are out of alignment with God's word, and out of alignment with His holy purposes for our states and for our nation. And what's sad is that most of the church and most of the people of our nation have bought into it. They bought into it "lock, stock, and barrel." They've eaten the poison. They're totally focused on an answer coming from a political or a governmental mindset. Government will not save this nation. The media will not save this nation. Educational systems cannot save this nation. The only thing that can bring salvation and the only thing that can bring victory to us is our Lord Jesus and His church – His Ekklesia! No, I'm not advocating that the Lord is going to take the president's position in the White House. Believe me, He doesn't want the president's position. His throne is much higher. It is exalted above all thrones. He is the King of kings and the Lord of lords, and we need to listen very carefully to him in this hour.

You need to get rid of religious biases and old political structures that have defined who you are and what you believe about the nation. We need the Lord to bring forth a revelation to His church and to His people about how He wants to transform, renew, and strengthen us into our original design as a nation. We've made a lot of mistakes, but the Lord is the one that forgives mistakes. We've done a lot of things that are full of injustice, but God is the one who holds justice in His hand. And He will bring forth the justice to our land that we've never seen before.

In the context of all of that, I want you to read from what was my daily readings this morning from Zechariah 3.

> *Then he showed me Joshua the high priest standing before the angel of the LORD, and Satan standing at his right hand to accuse him. The LORD said to Satan, "The LORD rebuke you, Satan! Indeed, the LORD who has chosen Jerusalem rebuke you! Is this not a brand plucked from the fire?" Now Joshua was clothed with filthy garments and standing before the angel. He spoke and said*

> to those who were standing before him, saying, "Remove the filthy garments from him." Again, he said to him, "See, I have taken your iniquity away from you and will clothe you with festal robes." Then I said, "Let them put a clean turban on his head." So, they put a clean turban on his head and clothed him with garments, while the angel of the LORD was standing by. And the angel of the LORD admonished Joshua, saying, "Thus says the LORD of hosts, 'If you will walk in My ways and if you will perform My service, then you will also govern My house and have charge of My courts, and I will grant you free access among these who are standing here.

Stop there. You can read it on further, because there is a tremendous promise that the Lord is giving to His people that He is here to wipe away our iniquities. Did we not just celebrate Good Friday and celebrate Resurrection, where the Lord moves with mighty glorious power to remove our iniquities, to remove our sins, and to destroy the power of sin, death, and the devil?

My friend Tim Sheets calls Satan or the devil the "forever loser," because he really is. He is forever losing. He stands next to us right now. He's trying to accuse us, trying to whisper his lies into us, and trying to whisper his plans and his strategies into us — whether individually, or as the church, or as the nation. The last thing that Satan wants is for a mighty victorious church or Ekklesia to rise up in this hour and say, "we've had enough."

We've had enough of the lies. We've had enough of the accusations. We've had enough of the unrighteousness and the injustices that are being released into our nation, our state, our churches and into our own personal lives. We've had enough. What's beautiful about this passage is that Joshua, who is clothed in filthy garments, is reclothed. He has new and pure vestments brought upon him; and now don't think of vestments here as some liturgical thing that we do in the Episcopal, Lutheran, Methodist, or Roman Catholic Church. The vestments here are garments of glory. They are garments that represent who we are as the chosen ones, the sons and daughters of the Most High God. We are kings and priests after His calling. He's given us new garments; He's put a new turban on our head. Much of this lines up with the words that Paul speaks when he says that we have put new armor on — the helmet of salvation, the belt of truth, the breastplate of righteousness, and the shield of faith. The Lord is clothing us.

Why do you think He clothes us with this, if we are just meant to sit in a pew for one hour on Sunday morning; hoping that we make it till Jesus comes? That is not who we are. We are standing in the presence of God. We are fully clothed in miraculous, glorious, and beautiful garments that He Himself has placed upon us. We have a fresh turban on our head. And now we have a fresh assignment. He says, "I'm giving you access. I'm giving you access to govern. I'm giving you access to be those that can speak as though speaking from the courts of heaven (tribunals) about what I want to happen in the days to come."

Satan may be standing right here accusing us as the forever loser, but you need to understand that that is not who we are in this hour. That is not what we are to listen to. We are to listen to the Spirit of the living God. We are to listen to Him who has clothed us in these garments. We have a mighty and victorious journey ahead of us. I'm expecting this nation to be saved. Again, it's not going to be saved by the Republicans or the Democrats. It's not going to be saved by the wisdom and human reasonings of man. It's going to be saved because we covenant ourselves as a nation back to God who is the one who clothes us. He brings us fully into His redemptive nature and design for us.

Stand there today knowing that you are fully clothed with the glory of the Lord. With a new turban on your head, you have access to not only listen to the spirit of God, but to speak out what He has said to your family, your job, your state, and to the nation. Blessings to all of you today. Don't listen to the forever loser.

Epilogue

And they overcame him because of the blood of the Lamb and because of the word of their testimony, and they did not love their life even when faced with death. (Revelation 12:11)

I want to turn your attention to words that have been written by Apostle Tim Sheets. He writes:

WORDS THAT YIELD HARVEST[18]

I decree God's word, in my mouth, will plant the heavens and the earth and I will see an abundant harvest.

"And I have put My words in your mouth; I have covered you with the shadow of My hand, that I may plant the heavens, lay the foundations of the earth, and say to Zion, 'You are My people'" (Isaiah 51:16 NKJV).

In this verse in Isaiah, God talks about words sounding forth from the mouths of His sons and daughters, His heirs, into the realm of the heavens or the earth. This again emphasizes that words are seeds—word seed decrees. This also includes prayer because prayers are words of communication seeded into the heavens and into the earth. Prayer is speech to God making a request, but it is also, at times, a decree of God's promises. Prayers express confidence in God's answering abilities, or they may ask for divine intervention into a situation. From the very beginning, God's original intent was for His sons and daughters, His heirs, to open their mouths and declare His words into the earth.

He has put His Word in your mouth so that He may plant it in the heavens and the earth. The word for plant is the Hebrew word nata, and it means "to plant, to fix, or to set in place" (Strong, H5193). God Himself was the original Gardener, and we have inherited that job from Him as His heirs. The entire

---

[18] Tim Sheets, <u>Prayers and Decrees that Activate Angel Armies</u>, page 88-89, Destiny Image Publishers, Inc.

universe is made to hearken to the voice of God's Word. Heaven and earth are made to respond to the voice of God's Word. Angel armies are made to respond to the voice of God's Word. Amazingly, human beings, made in God's image and likeness, are also carriers of God's voice when they are activated at the new birth. As His seed on the earth, we are to open our mouths and plant the heavens and the earth with God's Word.

We are to declare the words of God into the heavens and the earth, mankind, nations, government, congregations, and people everywhere to set in place foundations for stable government and society. We are to be stewards of what God said was to be. If the foundations are not set according to God's Word, then at some point that society is going to crumble under the weight of iniquitous roots. Jesus said that such a house will not be built upon rock; it will be built upon sand, and when the storm comes, it is going to fall (see Matt. 7: 26).

The Body of Christ is to open their mouths and plant God's Word into the earth. "I have put My words in your mouth that I might plant the heavens and the earth." Words are the seeds we plant with. JESUS, Your words still carry the greatest hope for humanity. Your words still create life and bring transformational change. Show me today how to declare Your Word into the culture around me. Fill my mouth with Your promises and give me wisdom as to how to plant Your Word with intentionality and courage."

As we come to the end of the book, I must again state emphatically that the Lord has raised up kings and priests, sons and daughters that are meant to be His representatives of His Kingdom on earth as it is in heaven. We must embrace this identity for it is the fullness of what He designed us to be from the very beginning of time. It was released into each one of us, like DNA, individually now of our conception. It became totally empowered in us as we came to faith in Jesus Christ, and now, as we say "yes" to His commands.

And let me state here that this won't be easy. The Lord has promised that we are in a war and that we will face horrific enemies who desire to do everything possible to destroy the mandates of our King. We must press on. We must go to the very end making sure that we are releasing His purpose into the Earth.

Let me also add this portion of Dutch Sheet's GiveHim15 that he wrote for March 23, 2023.

> I want to point out that America is now reaping horrible fruit from: 1) rejecting God and His ways; 2) willful sin and rebellion; 3) an uninformed populace

(including the church); and 4) electing dishonest, power-hungry, greedy, and incompetent leaders who have no fear of or respect for God.

These results include, but are not limited to:

- shocking levels of violence and crime
- gross immorality
- epidemic homelessness
- frighteningly low levels of learning, replaced by high levels of indoctrination
- out of control drug use causing record numbers of deaths
- open borders resulting in human trafficking, drugs flooding in that are killing hundreds of thousands of people, and untold numbers of terrorists, criminals, and spies entering America
- loss of freedoms
- a rewriting of our history
- a dual system of justice
- sickening but successful efforts to divide and polarize us
- a failing economy and skyrocketing debt
- disgusting abuse and mutilation of our children
- over 60 million abortions
- a weak military
- emboldened enemies planning to destroy us
- and more.

I am sharing these things, knowing you already see them; nothing I have said has surprised you. *But I want you to know I see them, as well - even as I declare revival and victory. I see them, even as I declare America shall be saved.* I am not in denial. But I don't allow them to erode my faith. I have watched this slow death of America taking place over the past 30-plus years, often grieving over the inability to awaken the American church, especially its leaders, to our true condition. America IS the proverbial frog in the kettle; we refused to wake up as the water grew warmer and warmer. Now it's boiling. And as a nation, we can no longer save ourselves; only a miracle from God can save us.

Here Is the Faith

But our God is a God of miracles! In His world dry bones - and dead frogs - can live again. The deadness of Abraham's and Sarah's bodies had nothing to do with whether Isaac was born. God has no problem overturning death with

His resurrection power. The question was whether their faith could embrace God's promise. Scripture and history have made clear that He is willing to use the prayers of a remnant to save nations. And a remnant of Americans is praying. We have powerful promises from Him that He is going to save our nation with an earthshaking revival.

Decree this daily! Appeal to His mercy, His grace, purchased with the blood of Christ. Appealing to heaven birthed our nation, and it will rebirth it. It still works! Be His voice of authority, releasing His Kingdom power and authority into our land. Stay engaged![19]

Everything regarding the Ekklesia is pointing us in the same direction. It's time to step it up. It's time to recognize our sonship and begin to move with courageous faith to decree forth God's power for transformation, reformation, and awakening. This is what tribunals are all about.

It Would Not Be Right

Now it just wouldn't be right if I did not somehow fit in some other Texas stuff in this message. I was in the process of finishing up the book when I came across this quote regarding David Crockett. Many of you know who he is. He came from Tennessee. But after a failed return to Congress, he declared, "Y'all can go to hell, but I'm going to Texas."

Sometimes I wonder if his timing was off because he came into Texas searching for a new place, a new destiny, and a new beginning for himself, his wife, and his family. He found land in the East Gate Region of our state near present day Honey Grove, Texas. But then he signed up to be a volunteer with the Texas Army and he started making his way south to see if he could meet up with General Sam Houston. His trip took him to San Antonio. There in San Antonio he became, along with his Tennesseans, one of the one hundred and eighty Texas patriots who were stationed inside the old shrine called the Alamo. After thirteen days of being besieged by a massive Mexican army under General Santa Anna, the Alamo fell and all of those inside, including Crockett, had died. I want you to read the following quote regarding Mr. Crockett.

> The Texas Quote of the Day is a description of David Crockett at the Alamo as told by a Mexican army officer:
>
> "A tall man, with flowing hair, was seen firing from the same place on the parapet during the entire siege. He wore a buckskin suit and a cap all of a pattern entirely different from those worn by his comrades. This man would

---

[19] Dutch Sheets, GiveHim15, March 23, 2023

kneel or lie down behind the low parapet, rest his long gun and fire, and we all learned to keep a good distance when he was seen to make ready to shoot. He rarely missed his mark, and when he fired, he almost always rose to his feet and calmly reloaded his gun, seemingly indifferent to the shots fired at him by our men. He had a strong, resonant voice and often railed at us, but as we did not understand English, we could not comprehend the import of the words, other than that they were defiant. This man I later learned was known as "Kwockey."

Captain Rafael Soldana of the Tampico Battalion

On Facebook, a blog posted by Traces of Texas records a story about another Alamo defender.

Everybody talks about Bowie, Travis, and Crockett but, to my way of thinking, James Butler Bonham was the most heroic. Bonham, who was boyhood friends with Travis in South Carolina (and whose whole reason for even being in Texas in the first place was because Travis had written him a letter the previous year that described a world of opportunity in Texas for enterprising young men like themselves), was sent by Travis to obtain aid for the garrison at Bexar on about February 16, 1836. He visited Goliad, but the commander of the forces there, James Fannin, was unable to provide assistance. Bonham's spirit is best described by T.R. Fehrenbach in his Texas opus, Lone Star: A History of Texas and the Texans:

"At the end, the weary Bonham, a lawyer, a Carolinian of exulted family and a friend of Travis, turned his mount around and rode back toward San Antonio. He was told it was useless to throw away his life. He answered back that Buck Travis deserved to know the answer to his appeals, spat upon the ground, and galloped west into his own immortality."

Thus, Bonham returned to the Alamo on March 3, riding through a hail of Mexican bullets to do it. Imagine being him as he approached the Alamo. He could certainly see the huge Mexican Army and must have known that he faced death either trying to get back inside or in the battle that would certainly follow. He could have turned his horse around, gone back to Goliad or Gonzales, and nobody would have ever known.

James Butler Bonham died in the battle of the Alamo on March 6, 1836, aged 29. He is believed to have died manning one of the cannons.

Why do I tell these stories? Because it marks the spirit of who we are as Texans. Yes, we can be called prideful and independent, but we are also a very passionate bunch, especially when the Spirit of living God has fallen upon us. It's time for us to rise up and be the instruments that God has desired us to be. We will bring forth His Kingdom and His will to earth. It might cost us our lives at the end, but that will be our testimony that we declared the purposes of God even to the point of death and stood firm in the midst of enemy fire.

You are a part of that call. Shuck off any remaining garments that you might have of religion and totally embrace the purposes of God being revealed in this hour regarding His Kingdom.

One last thing. The Lord always speaks to me in short questions or comments. He asked me not long ago, "Have you considered the onion?" I found it a quite interesting question, but I said, "tell me about it, Lord." He answered, "I want you to peel the onion, but I want you to know that when you have peeled the onion, there will be nothing left." He wants to make sure that there is nothing left of religion or our own selves, and that He has filled us completely with His spirit and His intentions.

Let's do this. It's time.

About the Author

Thomas Schlueter has been Pastor of Prince of Peace House of Prayer, a strategic house of prayer in Arlington Texas, since 1988. Pastor Schlueter obtained a Bachelor degree at Texas A&M University before receiving his Master of Divinity at Wartburg Theological Seminary. In 2008, the Lord commanded him to leave the Lutheran Church. At that time he was ordained again by Dr. Chuck Pierce and Glory of Zion Ministries in Denton. He received his Doctor of Ministry in July 2006 from Christian Leadership University in New York.

Dr. Schlueter's ministry extends beyond Prince of Peace House of Prayer and the Dallas-Fort Worth region. He is the Founder of Arlington Prayer Net, a network of prayer leaders from churches and ministries in Arlington and surrounding communities. The purpose of the network is to come alongside the pastoral staffs of local churches to start, strengthen and expand prayer ministries in the church.

He is the Apostolic Coordinator of the Texas Apostolic Prayer Network (TXAPN), which desires to see the redemptive anointing of the State to flow freely. They desire the people, the history, the culture, and the destiny of Texas to be transformed as the Lord is enthroned in our midst.

He is aligned with Apostle Dutch Sheets and his National Ekklesia International. He serves as the Texas and South-Central United States Regional Leader of the Reformation Prayer Network directed by Apostles Cindy and Mike Jacobs of Generals International. Dr. Schlueter is in covenant relationship with Dr. Chuck Pierce of Global Spheres International. Dr. Pierce set Dr. Schlueter in as coordinator of TXAPN in June of 2007. Pastor Schlueter teaches prayer and Bible seminars locally and internationally.

He is actively involved with praying strategically for city government and workplace ministry. He has a passion to see the whole city of Arlington, Texas, the State of Texas, and the United States come into their full redemptive purpose. He also has a zeal for developing a strong covenant relationship with the First Nations people. He desires to witness the releasing of the full destiny of God into their lives as the first peoples of our nation.

He is the author of <u>Return of the Priests,</u> a book declaring that God is restoring a kingdom of priests in our generation-not a priesthood defined by clerical collars and religious rituals. Rather it is a priesthood of everyday people walking intimately with

God, who act and speak with life-changing authority in their homes, neighborhoods, and workplaces.

He is also the author of Keeper of the Keys, a book that shares how God is opening doors so that His kingdom can come forth into this earth. But He needs gatekeepers – those who will open the doors of His power, presence and transforming life to come into family, workplace, city, state, and nation. You will discover in these pages that you are a Keeper of the Keys. He has empowered you to be a gatekeeper. Like Nehemiah and Peter, you have been given keys that will unlock the glory of the Lord in your region. It is also available on Amazon.

He is also the author of Wielding the Axe, a book that shares the story of how God has moved through Texas via the Texas Apostolic Prayer Network. The portals are open. The axe is sharpened. The oil is ready. The eagles have been released. The trumpet has sounded. Texas is going to war. Reveille has sounded. It's time to move. Set your face toward God and get ready to move into the new. In uncertain times, certainty! Expected the Unexpected! I've created a movement – you have been launched. You are no longer a network. You are a movement! Join the movement! We are wielding the axe and Texas is going to war!

He is married to Kay Sanders Schlueter, and they have three grown children: Josh and his fiancé Julie, Katie and her husband Tim, and Amy and her husband Allan. The couple has five grandchildren.

Contact:
Thomas Schlueter
Prince of Peace House of Prayer
Texas Apostolic Prayer Network
Arlington, Texas
pt4texas@gmail.com
www.texasapn.com or www.tomschlueter.com
YouTube: Dr. Tom Schlueter

OTHER BOOKS BY THE AUTHOR

These are available at Amazon in Paperback and Kindle

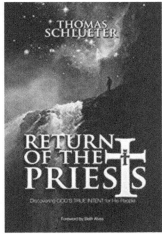

"To have the authority to bless and stand in for someone or some situation and not to do it is to miss the mark. To have the authority and not know it is a shame. Return of the Priests reveals the authority we must bless and stand in for people and situations and shows how to act on it. As an individual, a husband, a father, a grandfather, and a business owner, it is crucial for me to be the priest Jesus has called me to be."

Dick Bontke,
Owner of Gamma Engineering, Inc.

"Never have I read a book more needed by the Body of Christ. Return of the Priests is comprehensive, yet simple enough for all to grasp. May the revelation of our priesthood spoken of in this book cause a similar kind of a "religion quake" that Martin Luther's revelation stirred. This is a "must" book to read."

Olen Griffing, Presiding Apostle of Antioch Oasis International

When the time came to find someone to take apostolic/governmental prayer authority in Texas, Thomas Schlueter's name was presented to me. We met in Austin, and I presented him a large, golden key representing his authority in days ahead to influence this state, and consequently the nation. There is no one better to write a book like this than Thomas Schlueter. Not only does he operate in this authority, but the ability also to communicate the authority of a gatekeeper in his writing is incredible. A gate is a place of establishing authority. We each have gates in our life and spheres that the Lord has given us to rule over. This book will assist you in learning how to rule at your gate. Nehemiah is a wonderful picture of an administrative leader who moved to restore a broken city and establish new authority in that city. Keeper of the Keys is a transformational book that I highly recommend for every leader.

Dr. Chuck D. Pierce
President, Global Spheres Inc. President,
Glory of Zion International

Thomas Schlueter, pastor of Prince of Peace House of Prayer in Texas and statewide coordinator of the Texas Apostolic Prayer Network, understands the importance of being a gatekeeper for the Kingdom. Like a Nehemiah, he has received favor with city-wide, statewide, and national leaders who oversee gates of governmental leadership. Thomas also was a key helper in making sure that my work, Well Versed, was distributed to the entire Texas Legislature as well as to Governor Abbott, Lt. Governor Patrick, and Attorney General Paxton. It is a season of restoration and reformation in our nation, and Keeper of the Keys brings a thorough understanding of our role and responsibility as courageous restorers of the breach. The walls are being built. The gates are being restored. You are a keeper of keys, and this book will help ignite your passion for the task.

Dr. Jim Garlow
Senior Pastor of Skyline Church, San Diego

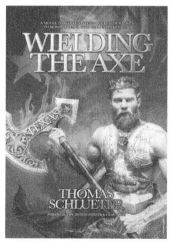

Finally, we have a book not only explaining the watchman but giving watchmen direction. God ordained us each to have a garden where we can watch and worship. For some, your garden is your home. For others, it might be your city, your state, or even your nation. His Ekklesia Kingdom leaders must stand in the gates and displace the authorities of hell that have somehow found their way to rule in positions of influence. In **Wielding the Axe**, Dr. Thomas Schlueter has created a wonderful manual to help us understand how our prayers become strategies for war. Ecclesiastes 10:10 speaks about the impact of a dull axe. As you read this book, get ready not only to sharpen your axe but to wield it in triumph ahead!

Dr. Chuck D. Pierce, Apostle
President, Glory of Zion International Ministries
President, Global Spheres, Inc.

Made in the USA
Middletown, DE
28 February 2025

71899569R00057